Webpack Unleashed
A Thorough Exploration of Module Bundling

Adam Jones

Contents

Preface

In an era where the web has become the backbone of digital interaction and innovation, the complexity of building efficient, scalable, and maintainable applications has grown exponentially. As the architecture of web applications advances, so too do the tools that aid in their development. Enter Webpack, a powerful module bundler that has revolutionized the way we assemble and optimize our web applications. This book, "Webpack Unleashed: A Thorough Exploration of Module Bundling," is your comprehensive guide to mastering the intricacies of this indispensable tool.

The genesis of Webpack lies in its ability to transform the process of managing assets in web applications, offering developers the flexibility to combine, transform, and integrate files from different sources. Its importance in the modern web development toolkit cannot be overstated, as it addresses both the complexities of module bundling and the growing demands for performance and efficiency.

This book endeavors to provide a deep dive into the world of Webpack, laying bare its underlying mechanics and showcasing its powerful capabilities. A meticulous exploration of configuration, loader and plugin integration, code splitting, tree shaking, and optimization strategies will empower developers with the skills needed to harness the full potential of Webpack. Furthermore, readers will gain insights into advanced patterns and techniques for managing complex applications, deploying optimized builds, and leveraging the latest functionalities introduced in newer versions of

Webpack.

Structured with the reader's learning journey in mind, "Webpack Unleashed" is divided into chapters that systematically cover the progressive layers of Webpack. From foundational concepts in the initial chapters—designed to equip beginners with essential knowledge—to more advanced discussions in later sections that cater to experienced developers, the book scales in complexity to enlighten and equip its audience comprehensively.

To bridge the gap between theory and practice, the book is rich in practical examples, real-world scenarios, and best practices. This approach ensures that readers not only understand the theoretical aspects of Webpack but also how to apply them to real projects effectively.

This book serves as an essential resource for all web developers, from those who are just starting their journey with module bundlers to seasoned professionals seeking to refine and modernize their approach to web application development. By the end of this exploration, readers will have acquired a robust and nuanced understanding of Webpack, enabling them to meet the evolving challenges of web development with competence and assurance.

Whether you are on a quest to enhance your professional capabilities or are simply intrigued by the art and science of bundling, "Webpack Unleashed" invites you to discover, learn, and master the dynamic world of Webpack. Welcome to a realm where your web development skills are limited only by your imagination.

Chapter 1

Introduction to Webpack: Understanding the Basics

Webpack is a powerful module bundler that has become an indispensable tool in the development of complex web applications. It processes applications by recursively building a dependency graph that includes every module your project needs, then packages all of those modules into a small number of bundles - often just one - to be loaded by the browser. This chapter lays the foundation by explaining the core concepts of Webpack, including its functionality, advantages, and the role it plays in modern web development ecosystems. It provides a solid starting point for those new to Webpack and seeks to familiarize readers with the terminology and fundamental principles that underpin more advanced topics covered later in this guidebook.

1.1 What is Webpack and Why Use It?

Webpack is a module bundler, but to fully appreciate its utility, it is essential to understand what this term means in the context of web development. At its core, Webpack takes modules with dependencies and generates static assets representing those modules. This is a fundamental task as modern web applications rely on a complex structure of JavaScript, CSS, images, and font files, among others.

The problem Webpack solves is multifaceted. First, loading each file individually in a web application is inefficient. Each file request incurs a performance penalty due to the overhead of HTTP requests. Bundling seeks to mitigate this by combining many files into fewer packages, thus reducing the number of requests needed during page load. Secondly, managing dependencies manually in large projects is error-prone and challenging. Webpack automatically resolves these dependencies, ensuring that files are loaded in the correct order.

The reasons for using Webpack can be encapsulated in the following points:

- **Optimization:** Webpack optimizes the bundling process, ensuring that only what is necessary is sent to the client. This optimization includes tree-shaking, a process of removing unused code, and code-splitting, which allows breaking the codebase into smaller chunks loaded on demand.

- **Development Efficiency:** Through features like hot module replacement, developers can see their changes reflected in the browser without needing a full reload, greatly accelerating the development workflow.

- **Flexibility:** Webpack provides a high level of customization through loaders and plugins, making it possible to tailor the build process to the specific needs of a project, from transpiling newer JavaScript syntax to backwards-compatible code, to processing images and styles.

- **Consistency:** By serving as the central hub for all resources in an application, Webpack ensures that resources are consistently processed, resulting in predictable and reliable output.

One of Webpack's strong suits is its ability to handle more than just JavaScript. By employing loaders, Webpack can manage other resources such as CSS, LESS, SASS, and images, allowing for a more cohesive and integrated approach to handling assets. This transforms the bundling process from a simple concatenation of scripts into a sophisticated pipeline that can handle a vast array of web development tasks, enhancing both the development experience and the performance of the final application.

To illustrate a basic Webpack setup, consider the following configuration code:

```
1   const path = require('path');
2
3   module.exports = {
4       entry: './src/index.js',
5       output: {
6           filename: 'bundle.js',
7           path: path.resolve(__dirname, 'dist'),
8       },
9   };
```

This simple Webpack configuration specifies an entry point ('src/index.js'), where the bundling process begins. It follows the dependencies defined in this entry point to bundle the necessary modules together into 'bundle.js', which is output into the 'dist' directory. This setup exemplifies Webpack's basic functionality, laying the groundwork for more advanced techniques and optimizations that will be discussed in subsequent sections.

In summary, Webpack's role in modern web development cannot be overstated. Its ability to bundle various assets, optimize the loading process, and streamline development workflows makes it an indispensable tool in the creation of efficient, maintainable, and high-performing web applications.

1.2   Core Concepts of Webpack

Webpack integrates into the development process as a module bundler, a tool which vastly simplifies the task of managing dependencies and modules in web projects. The essence of Webpack revolves around several core concepts, which are pivotal in grasping its utility and functionality. These include entry points, output properties, loaders, plugins, and mode configuration. Each of these concepts plays a critical role in the bundling process, influencing how Webpack operates and delivers the final bundled assets.

Entry Points: At the heart of every Webpack configuration is the entry point. Entry points signify the modules where the bundling process starts. They act as roots of the dependency graph that Webpack constructs. By default, Webpack looks for the ./src/index.js file as the starting point of an application, but this can be customized as per project requirements. The entry point property in a Webpack configuration, denoted as entry, can be a simple string pointing to a single file or an object specifying multiple entry points for more complex setups. The syntax for defining an entry point is illustrated below:

```
1  module.exports = {
2    entry: './path/to/my/entry/file.js'
3  };
```

Output Properties: The output property in a Webpack configuration dictates where the bundled assets will be emitted, and what they will be named. It is an object that specifies the target directory and the naming pattern for the output file(s). The path attribute within the output property defines the directory for storing the bundled files, while the filename attribute specifies the name of the generated bundle. For a basic setup, the output configuration could be structured as follows:

```
1  const path = require('path');
2
3  module.exports = {
4    output: {
5      path: path.resolve(__dirname, 'dist'),
6      filename: 'bundle.js'
7    }
8  };
```

Loaders: Webpack by itself only understands JavaScript. Loaders allow Webpack to process other types of files and convert them into valid modules that can be included in the output bundles. This is crucial for handling a wide variety of assets such as stylesheets, images, and HTML files, making loaders an indispensable feature of Webpack. Loaders are configured within the module.rules array of the Webpack configuration, specifying test patterns for file types and the loaders to apply. An example configuring a loader for CSS files is provided below:

```
1   module.exports = {
2     module: {
3       rules: [
4         {
5           test: /\.css$/,
6           use: ['style-loader', 'css-loader']
7         }
8       ]
9     }
10  };
```

Plugins: While loaders transform individual files, plugins offer a broader range of capabilities. They can be utilized for a variety of tasks such as bundle optimization, asset management, and environment variable injection. Plugins are instantiated within the plugins array of the Webpack configuration, and they have access to the entire Webpack build process. An example of utilizing a plugin to generate an HTML file that includes the output bundle is as follows:

```
1   const HtmlWebpackPlugin = require('html-webpack-plugin');
2
3   module.exports = {
4     plugins: [
5       new HtmlWebpackPlugin({
6         title: 'My Awesome Application',
7         template: './src/index.html'
8       })
9     ]
10  };
```

Mode: Webpack's mode configuration supports three settings: development, production, and none. Setting the mode informs Webpack to use corresponding default configurations that optimize the build based on the specified environment. The development mode facilitates debugging and faster builds, whereas the production mode enables optimizations like tree shaking, uglification, and minification to produce efficient output bundles. The mode can be set directly within the Webpack configuration as shown below:

```
1   module.exports = {
```

```
2    mode: 'development'
3  };
```

Understanding these core concepts is crucial for effectively leveraging Webpack in web development projects. They allow developers to configure Webpack tailored to specific project needs, optimizing both the development process and the performance of the final application.

1.3   The   Role   of   Bundlers   in   Web Development

The evolution of web applications from simple, static pages to complex, highly interactive applications has necessitated a shift in web development practices. Historically, developers would include scripts in websites by directly linking to individual JavaScript files. However, as applications grew in complexity, this approach became inefficient. Bundlers, such as Webpack, emerged as a solution to this problem, playing a crucial role in modern web development by optimizing the delivery of web resources.

One primary function of a bundler is to aggregate various resources, including JavaScript, CSS, and images, into fewer files. This aggregation significantly reduces the number of HTTP requests needed to load a web application, which directly impacts load times. In an era where performance and speed are paramount, the role of bundlers in enhancing web application efficiency cannot be overstated.

- Bundlers minimize server requests by combining multiple files into a bundle.

- They enable modular development by allowing developers to write modular code that is then efficiently compiled.

- Bundlers optimize resources through minification and uglification, further improving application performance.

16

- They allow for the use of next-generation JavaScript features through transpilation, ensuring compatibility across different browsers.

- Additionally, bundlers facilitate the incorporation of environment-specific settings, allowing developers to tailor their code for development or production environments efficiently.

The effectiveness of bundlers extends beyond file aggregation to include sophisticated transformations and optimizations. For instance, Webpack employs a technique known as tree shaking to eliminate unused code from the final bundle. This process not only reduces the size of the output file but also enhances the overall performance of the web application.

Let's consider an example where Webpack is used to bundle a simple web application. The project structure consists of several JavaScript modules and CSS files.

```
1  // index.js
2  import { add } from './math.js';
3  console.log(add(1, 2));
4
5  // math.js
6  export const add = (a, b) => a + b;
7  export const subtract = (a, b) => a - b;
```

Without a bundler, these files would need to be included separately in the HTML document, creating additional HTTP requests. By utilizing Webpack, developers can consolidate these dependencies into a single output file, significantly streamlining the loading process.

```
Compiled successfully. Bundle size: 1.24KB
```

Webpack's configuration file, typically named `webpack.config.js`, plays a pivotal role in defining the bundling process. It specifies entry points, output configurations, loaders, plugins, and other essential parameters guiding how the application's resources are processed and bundled.

```
1  // webpack.config.js example
```

```
2   const path = require('path');
3
4   module.exports = {
5     entry: './src/index.js',
6     output: {
7       path: path.resolve(__dirname, 'dist'),
8       filename: 'bundle.js'
9     }
10  };
```

This configuration file directs Webpack to begin bundling at
./src/index.js, process the required modules, and output the
final bundle as bundle.js in the dist directory.

Bundlers like Webpack play an indispensable role in modern web
development. They streamline the web development process by
efficiently managing and optimizing web resources. This not only
eases the developer's workload but also significantly improves the
performance and user experience of web applications. As the
complexity of web applications continues to grow, the importance
of understanding and leveraging bundlers cannot be understated.

1.4   Understanding Entry Points

Let's explore the concept of entry points within the context of Webpack. An entry point in Webpack serves as the initial starting point
for the bundling process. It is fundamentally a module, which Webpack uses to commence the construction of the internal dependency
graph. This graph is a structured representation of all the modules
and assets your application requires, delineated based on their inter-
dependencies. Designating an entry point is vital as it signals to Webpack where to start and which modules or files to encompass in the
bundle it produces.

To specify an entry point, one must make use of the entry property in
the Webpack configuration file, usually named webpack.config.js.
This property is flexible, catering to single or multiple entry points,
depending on the structure and necessities of your project.

```
1   module.exports = {
2     entry: './path/to/my/entry/file.js'
```

```
3   };
```

In the above example, the `entry` property is set to a string that specifies the path to the entry file. This approach is suitable for single-page applications where a solitary entry point suffices.

For more complex scenarios, involving multiple entry points to cater to various parts of an application, an object notation is used. This allows for the definition of multiple named entry points.

```
1   module.exports = {
2     entry: {
3       app: './path/to/app/entry/file.js',
4       admin: './path/to/admin/entry/file.js'
5     }
6   };
```

In this configuration, two entry points are defined: `app` and `admin`. Each property's key serves as the name of the entry point, while the value is the path to the respective entry file. This approach is beneficial for multi-page applications, enabling specific bundles to be created for different parts of the application, hence optimizing load times and resource utilization.

Understanding the role of entry points and correctly configuring them is fundamental to harnessing the full capabilities of Webpack. It influences not only the structure of the generated bundles but also the efficiency of the bundling process. Moreover, appropriate entry point configuration can significantly impact the performance of your application, as it determines how resources are loaded and utilized in the browser.

To grasp the practical implications of entry points, consider their effect on the generation of the dependency graph. When Webpack processes the specified entry file, it identifies all dependencies of that module, including other modules and assets like images or CSS files. It then recursively processes each dependency in turn, constructing a comprehensive graph that captures the entirety of what's required to execute the application. The accuracy and effectiveness of this process hinge on the thoughtful designation of entry points.

Hence, the selection of entry points is not merely a technical decision but a strategic one that influences the architecture and performance of your application. Careful consideration should be given to how your project is structured and how different modules interrelate to ensure that the entry points you choose aptly reflect the composition and needs of your application.

1.5   Exploring Output Properties

Let's dive into the output properties in Webpack, which are pivotal for determining how and where the bundles generated by Webpack should be outputted. The output property in a Webpack configuration is an object that dictates various aspects like the destination directory for the output bundle, the name of the output file, and other critical features such as public path settings.

To start, the output property is defined within the Webpack configuration file, typically named `webpack.config.js`. This property is an object that contains various settings. One of the most crucial settings within this object is the `path` property, which specifies the output directory for the bundle(s). The `path` property requires an absolute path, which can be constructed using Node.js's `path` module. Here's an example:

```
1  const path = require('path');
2
3  module.exports = {
4    output: {
5      path: path.resolve(__dirname, 'dist'),
6    },
7  };
```

In the code above, the `path.resolve()` method is used to generate an absolute path to the `dist` directory relative to the current directory (`__dirname`). This designates `dist` as the directory where Webpack will output the bundled files.

Another crucial property within the output object is `filename`. This property defines the name of the single output file for your bundle. This is especially useful in scenarios where your project results in a single bundle. An example configuration is as follows:

```
module.exports = {
  output: {
    filename: 'bundle.js',
  },
};
```

In the example above, the output bundle will be named bundle.js. It's important to note that the filename property can also include patterns, such as [name] or [hash], to dynamically generate names based on the entry point names or a unique hash generated for each build, respectively.

For projects that may result in multiple bundles, filename can be configured to dynamically generate the names based on the entry point that generated the bundle. This is achieved using placeholders such as [name] within the filename string, as illustrated in the following snippet:

```
module.exports = {
  output: {
    filename: '[name].bundle.js',
  },
};
```

In addition to path and filename, the publicPath property plays a significant role. This property is used to specify the public URL of the output directory when referenced in a browser. For example, if your application is hosted under a specific path on your server, publicPath can be set to this path so that Webpack can correctly reference the bundles. An example setting is shown below:

```
module.exports = {
  output: {
    publicPath: '/assets/',
  },
};
```

In the configuration above, the publicPath is set to /assets/, which instructs Webpack to prepend /assets/ to all asset URLs in the generated output bundles.

Understanding and configuring the output properties correctly is vital for ensuring that the Webpack-generated bundles are named and placed as desired, and are correctly referenced within your web application. This foundational knowledge sets the stage for more advanced configurations and optimizations that will be explored in subsequent chapters.

1.6 Working with Loaders and Plugins: An Overview

Webpack's core functionality can be extended with the use of loaders and plugins, two powerful tools that enable developers to process different types of files and enhance the bundling process. This section will discuss the definitions, differences, and how to effectively utilize loaders and plugins in a Webpack configuration.

Loaders in Webpack transform the files before they are added to the dependency graph. They are responsible for loading the source code of various file types and converting them into JavaScript modules. Since Webpack only understands JavaScript, loaders play a pivotal role in handling non-JavaScript files such as CSS, HTML, and image files. A loader is essentially a function that takes the source file as an input and returns it in a format that Webpack can manipulate.

The configuration for loaders in Webpack is specified using the `module.rules` array. Each rule contains conditions under which a specific loader will be applied. The following is a basic example of using a loader:

```
1   module.exports = {
2     module: {
3       rules: [
4         {
5           test: /\.css$/,
6           use: ['style-loader', 'css-loader']
7         }
8       ]
9     }
10  };
```

This configuration applies the `css-loader` to import CSS files into JavaScript files, and then the `style-loader` to inject the styles into the DOM.

Plugins, on the other hand, offer a wider range of capabilities than loaders. They can be used to perform a broad array of tasks like bundle optimization, asset management, and environment variable injection. Plugins have access to the entire Webpack build process, making them incredibly powerful for complex configurations. A plugin is applied by adding a new instance of it to the `plugins` array in the Webpack configuration file.

The following example demonstrates how to use the `HtmlWebpackPlugin` to generate an HTML file that includes all your webpack bundles:

```
1   const HtmlWebpackPlugin = require('html-webpack-plugin');
2
3   module.exports = {
4     plugins: [
5       new HtmlWebpackPlugin({
6         title: 'My Application',
7         template: './src/index.html'
8       })
9     ]
10  };
```

Unlike loaders, which are applied on a per-file basis, plugins apply to the entire build process.

To summarize, loaders and plugins are essential for extending Webpack's capabilities. Loaders allow processing and conversion of different file types, while plugins can be used to customize the build process. Understanding how to configure and use loaders and plugins is critical for optimizing your Webpack setup.

1.7 The Webpack Configuration File: A First Look

At the heart of Webpack's functionality is its configuration file, typically named `webpack.config.js`. This JavaScript file is a key element because it tells Webpack exactly how to behave when executing its bundling process. To grasp the power of Webpack, understanding the structure and syntax of this configuration file is essential. This section provides a comprehensive introduction to the components of the webpack.config.js file and how they influence the bundling process.

The webpack.config.js file is structured as a JavaScript module, exporting an object that Webpack can interpret. This object contains properties that define different aspects of the Webpack process, such as entry points, output configurations, loaders, plugins, and more. Let's break down these properties for a better understanding.

Entry

The entry property is where the process begins. It specifies the entry point or points for the application. This is where Webpack starts building its internal dependency graph. The entry property can be a simple string pointing to a single file or an object specifying multiple entry points. Here is an example:

```
1  module.exports = {
2    entry: './path/to/my/entry/file.js'
3  };
```

For multiple entry points, the configuration might look like this:

```
1  module.exports = {
2    entry: {
3      app: './src/app.js',
4      admin: './src/admin.js'
5    }
6  };
```

Output

The output property tells Webpack where to emit the bundles it creates and how to name these files. It defaults to ./dist/main.js for the main output file and to the ./dist folder for other generated files. Here is a basic output configuration:

```
1  module.exports = {
2    //...
```

```
3    output: {
4      filename: 'bundle.js',
5      path: __dirname + '/dist'
6    }
7  };
```

This configuration would output the bundle to a file named bundle.js in the dist directory.

Loaders

Loaders in Webpack transform the files before adding them to the bundle. Since Webpack only understands JavaScript and JSON files, loaders allow the bundling of other types of files, converting them into modules that can be included in your application's dependency graph. The configuration below shows how to use loaders for CSS files:

```
1  module.exports = {
2    //...
3    module: {
4      rules: [
5        {
6          test: /\.css$/,
7          use: [
8            'style-loader',
9            'css-loader'
10         ]
11       }
12     ]
13   }
14 };
```

This tells Webpack to use the css-loader to process .css files and the style-loader to inject the style into the DOM.

Plugins

Plugins are the backbone of Webpack's extensibility, allowing you to perform a wide range of tasks like bundle optimization, asset management, and environment variable injection. They can be included by requiring the plugin and adding it to the plugins array in the configuration object. Below is an example of using the

`HtmlWebpackPlugin`:

```
const HtmlWebpackPlugin = require('html-webpack-plugin');

module.exports = {
  //...
  plugins: [
    new HtmlWebpackPlugin({
      template: './src/index.html'
    })
  ]
};
```

This plugin automatically generates an HTML file for your bundle, or uses an existing template if specified.

Understanding the `webpack.config.js` file's structure and options is crucial for leveraging Webpack's full potential. This file acts as a roadmap, guiding Webpack through the complex process of transforming and bundling your application's assets. The examples provided above represent only a fraction of Webpack's capabilities, serving as a starting point for deeper exploration into the tool's extensive configuration options.

In the subsequent sections, we will delve into each aspect of Webpack's configuration in more detail, providing a comprehensive understanding that will enable fine-tuned control over the bundling process.

1.8 Dependencies: Node.js and NPM

Before delving into setting up Webpack, it is crucial to understand its two primary dependencies: Node.js and the Node Package Manager (NPM). These components are fundamental to the functionality of Webpack, serving as the platform and the marketplace for managing the packages or modules that Webpack bundles.

Node.js

Node.js is a runtime environment that allows you to run JavaScript on the server side. It is built on Chrome's V8 JavaScript engine, which compiles JavaScript directly to native machine code. This enables JavaScript to run with performance characteristics comparable to other compiled languages like C++ or Java.

Node.js is used not just for server-side applications but also in building development tools like Webpack. It provides a rich library of various JavaScript modules which simplifies the development of web applications.

Verifying Node.js Installation

To use Webpack, you must first ensure that Node.js is installed on your development machine. This can be verified by opening your command line or terminal and typing the following commands:

```
1  node -v
2  npm -v
```

The above commands should return the versions of Node.js and NPM installed on your system. If Node.js is not installed, it will return an error message prompting you to install it.

Installing Node.js

In the event that Node.js is not installed, you can download the installer from the Node.js official website (https://nodejs.org). It is recommended to download the LTS (Long Term Support) version for better stability. The installation process is straightforward and will automatically include NPM, which is bundled with Node.js.

NPM (Node Package Manager)

NPM is the world's largest software registry, containing over 800,000 code packages. Developers use NPM to share and borrow packages, and many organizations also use NPM to manage private development as well. It comes pre-installed with Node.js, which means once you have Node.js installed, you can start using NPM immediately.

Understanding NPM for Webpack

When working with Webpack, NPM plays a critical role in managing the project's dependencies. It allows you to install, share, and manage the lifecycle of dependencies in your projects, such as libraries and frameworks.

To install Webpack using NPM, you would use the following command:

```
1   npm install webpack webpack-cli --save-dev
```

This command installs the 'webpack' and 'webpack-cli' packages as a development dependency in your project, which means they will be used during the development phase but not included in the production build.

package.json: The Heart of Any Node.js Project

The package.json file in a Node.js project contains metadata relevant to the project. This file is used for managing the project's dependencies, scripts, version and much more. When you install a package using NPM, a package.json file is automatically generated or updated in your project directory, listing the installed packages under the "dependencies" or "devDependencies" section.

In summary, understanding and managing Node.js and NPM is fundamental for setting up Webpack in your project. Node.js serves as the runtime environment, while NPM is used to manage the packages that your project depends on, including Webpack itself.

1.9 Installing and Setting Up Webpack

Installing and setting up Webpack in a project is a straightforward process, provided that the necessary prerequisites are in place. Before initiating the installation, it is essential to ensure that Node.js and npm (Node Package Manager) are installed on the development machine. Node.js serves as the runtime environment for executing JavaScript code outside of a web browser, while npm acts as a package manager that facilitates the installation of libraries and tools needed for modern web development, including Webpack.

To verify the installation of Node.js and npm, execute the following commands in your terminal or command prompt:

```
node -v
npm -v
```

These commands will display the installed versions of Node.js and npm, respectively. If the commands return versions, it confirms that both Node.js and npm are installed correctly. If not, it is necessary to download and install Node.js from the official website, which automatically includes npm.

With Node.js and npm installed, the next step is to create a new directory for the project or navigate to an existing project directory where Webpack will be added. Once inside the project directory, initialize a new npm project by running the following command:

```
npm init -y
```

This command creates a package.json file in the project directory, which is crucial for managing project dependencies, scripts, and version information. The -y flag automatically fills in default values without prompting for input.

After initializing the npm project, Webpack can be installed using npm. Webpack consists of the core webpack package and the webpack-cli package, which provides a set of command-line interface tools for working with Webpack configurations. Install both packages as development dependencies by executing the following command:

```
1   npm install --save-dev webpack webpack-cli
```

The --save-dev flag specifies that these packages are development dependencies, which means they are used in the development process but not required in the production environment.

Upon successful installation, the webpack and webpack-cli packages, along with their versions, will be listed under the devDependencies section of the package.json file. This concludes the installation process.

To verify the installation of Webpack, run:

```
1   npx webpack --version
```

This command will display the installed version of Webpack, indicating that Webpack is set up correctly and ready to be used in the project.

With Webpack installed, the next step is configuring it to suit the project's specific needs, which involves creating a webpack.config.js file in the project root. This file is where various configurations, such as entry points, output settings, loaders, and plugins, are defined. A basic Webpack configuration is shown below:

```
1   const path = require('path');
2
3   module.exports = {
4     entry: './src/index.js',
5     output: {
6       path: path.resolve(__dirname, 'dist'),
7       filename: 'bundle.js'
8     }
9   };
```

This configuration specifies the entry point of the application ('./src/index.js') and the output file ('bundle.js') that Webpack will generate in the dist directory. This setup serves as a foundation for more complex configurations involving loaders and plugins, which are covered in subsequent sections.

Webpack installation and basic setup introduce developers to the seamless integration of Webpack into their web development workflow, allowing them to leverage its powerful bundling capabilities.

1.10   Creating Your First Webpack Project

Creating a new Webpack project requires the prior installation of Node.js and npm (Node Package Manager) as they form the foundation for running Webpack. Assuming these dependencies are set up, we will proceed step by step to initialize and configure a basic Webpack project.

Step 1: Project Initialization

Begin by creating a new directory for your project and navigating into it using the terminal. Execute the following commands:

```
1   mkdir my-webpack-project
2   cd my-webpack-project
```

Once inside the project directory, initialize a new npm package:

```
1   npm init -y
```

This command generates a package.json file with default settings, which will track project dependencies.

Step 2: Installing Webpack and Webpack CLI

Webpack and its Command Line Interface (CLI) are essential tools for working with Webpack. Install them as devDependencies:

```
1   npm install webpack webpack-cli --save-dev
```

This command updates the package.json file, listing Webpack and the Webpack CLI as development dependencies.

Step 3: Configuring the Webpack

Create a file named webpack.config.js in the project root. This file exports an object that configures Webpack. A basic configuration includes properties for *entry*, *output*, and *mode*:

31

```
1   const path = require('path');
2
3   module.exports = {
4     entry: './src/index.js',
5     output: {
6       filename: 'bundle.js',
7       path: path.resolve(__dirname, 'dist'),
8     },
9     mode: 'development',
10  };
```

The entry property specifies the entry point file, output defines where to emit the bundles and how to name them, and mode sets the mode to either *development*, *production*, or *none*.

Step 4: Creating the Entry Point File

Inside your project, create a src directory with an index.js file:

```
1   mkdir src
2   echo console.log('Hello, Webpack!') > src/index.js
```

This index.js file will serve as the entry point for Webpack, which will process any dependencies starting from it.

Step 5: Building the Project

With the configuration in place, build the project by running the following npm script:

```
1   npx webpack
```

This command processes the input as specified in webpack.config.js and generates the output in the dist directory. After successful completion, the dist folder should contain the bundle.js file.

Step 6: Viewing the Bundle in a Browser

To view the results, create an HTML file named index.html inside the dist directory:

```
1   <!DOCTYPE html>
2   <html>
3   <head>
4     <title>Webpack Project</title>
5   </head>
6   <body>
```

```
7   <script src="bundle.js"></script>
8   </body>
9   </html>
```

Opening index.html in a browser will execute the code in bundle.js, displaying the console message defined in src/index.js.

By following these steps, you have successfully set up and built a basic Webpack project. This foundation can be expanded to include more complex configurations, loaders, and plugins, as will be discussed in subsequent sections.

1.11   An Overview of the Webpack Ecosystem

The Webpack ecosystem is an extensive network of tools, plugins, loaders, and community contributions that enhance the core functionality of Webpack. Understanding the ecosystem is crucial for effectively leveraging Webpack in web development projects. This ecosystem can be seen as an interconnected structure that supports a wide array of development needs, from simple asset management to complex code transformation and optimization processes.

Loaders

Webpack itself only understands JavaScript. Loaders transform other types of files into modules that can be included in your project's dependency graph. Commonly used loaders include:

- style-loader and css-loader - transform CSS files into modules so they can be imported into JavaScript files.

- file-loader - processes files like images and fonts and outputs them into the build directory.

- babel-loader - transpiles ES6 and JSX syntax to ensure compatibility with older browsers.

Each loader can be configured with options to customize its processing. Loaders can be chained to process files through multiple steps.

Plugins

Plugins are the backbone of the Webpack ecosystem, offering a vast range of solutions for customization and automation of the build process. They have more comprehensive access to Webpack's internal processes compared to loaders. Notable plugins in the ecosystem include:

- `HtmlWebpackPlugin` - simplifies the creation of HTML files to serve your webpack bundles.

- `CleanWebpackPlugin` - removes/cleans your build folder(s) before building.

- `MiniCssExtractPlugin` - extracts CSS into separate files. It creates a CSS file per JS file which contains CSS.

- `UglifyJsPlugin` - minimizes JavaScript files using UglifyJS.

Custom plugins can be created to extend Webpack's capabilities even further, encompassing everything from performance optimizations to the generation of custom asset attributes.

Webpack Dev Server

`Webpack Dev Server` enhances the development workflow by providing a live reloading server and simplifying the development of single-page applications. It can be configured to automatically reload the page or to hot module replace parts of the page without a full reload when changes are made to the source code. This feature significantly improves the development experience by offering instant feedback on code changes.

Webpack Configuration File

The webpack.config.js file is the heart of any Webpack project. It specifies the entry and output points, rules for how different file types should be processed, plugins to be used, and many other important settings. A solid understanding of this configuration file is essential for effective use of Webpack. The file allows for granular control over the build process, enabling developers to tailor the build to the specific needs of their project.

Community and Contributions

The Webpack ecosystem is supported by a vibrant community. Numerous tutorials, guides, plugins, and loaders are available and contributed by developers around the world. This collective effort continually expands the capabilities of Webpack, ensuring it remains at the forefront of module bundling solutions for modern web development.

The Webpack ecosystem offers an extensive array of tools and configurations to streamline the web development process. From loaders and plugins improving the handling of various asset types to the Webpack Dev Server enhancing the development workflow, the ecosystem provides the building blocks for efficient, optimized web application development. By understanding and utilizing these tools, developers can significantly enhance the performance and maintainability of their web projects.

Chapter 2

Configuring Webpack: Core Concepts

The configuration file is the heart of a Webpack setup, determining how modules are processed, bundled, and optimized. This chapter delves into creating and tailoring the Webpack configuration to meet specific project requirements. It covers essential concepts such as entry points, output, loaders, plugins, and resolves, providing clear examples and advice on how to effectively use these configurations to control the behavior of Webpack. By understanding these core concepts, developers can leverage Webpack's full potential to streamline and enhance their development workflow.

2.1 Deep Dive into Webpack Configuration

Webpack's configuration file is essentially a JavaScript file that exports an object. This object defines various options which tell Webpack how to behave. Given its pivotal role, understanding each aspect of this configuration is crucial for effective development.

Let's start with the basic structure of a Webpack configuration file. Typically named `webpack.config.js`, this file resides at the root of the project directory. The simplest version of this file could look something like this:

```
1  const path = require('path');
2
3  module.exports = {
4    entry: './src/index.js',
5    output: {
6      filename: 'bundle.js',
7      path: path.resolve(__dirname, 'dist'),
8    },
9  };
```

In this basic example, two primary properties are defined: `entry` and `output`.

- The `entry` property signifies the entry point of the application, instructing Webpack from where it should start bundling the modules. In many applications, this starting point is the `index.js` file, but it can be configured to any file or files as per project requirements.

- The `output` property instructs Webpack on where to emit the bundles it creates and how to name these files. Here, `filename` defines the name of the output file, and `path` specifies the absolute path to the directory where the output file should be generated.

Understanding the significance of the `entry` and `output` properties lays the foundation for mastering Webpack's configuration. However, the real power of Webpack manifests when utilizing its rich set of options like `loaders`, `plugins`, and `resolve`.

Loaders in Webpack allow the processing of other types of files besides JavaScript, transforming them into valid modules that can be utilized in your application's runtime. This might include converting SASS to CSS, transpiling TypeScript to JavaScript, or even converting images into data URLs. Configuring loaders involves specifying a `test` property (to identify which files should be transformed)

and a use property (to determine which loader should be used) like
so:

```
module: {
  rules: [
    {
      test: /\.css$/,
      use: [
        'style-loader',
        'css-loader',
      ],
    },
  ],
}
```

This configuration for instance allows Webpack to handle CSS files
by first converting CSS into JavaScript (using `css-loader`) and then
injecting the resulting styles dynamically into the page (using
`style-loader`).

Plugins serve a broader purpose, assisting in tasks ranging from
bundle optimization and asset management to environment
variable injection. Incorporating a plugin into your build process
typically involves importing the plugin module at the top of your
configuration file and then adding a new instance of the plugin to
the plugins array. For example, to use the `HtmlWebpackPlugin` for
generating a base HTML file and injecting the output bundle
automatically, the configuration would include:

```
const HtmlWebpackPlugin = require('html-webpack-plugin');

plugins: [
  new HtmlWebpackPlugin({
    title: 'Webpack App',
    template: './src/index.html',
  }),
]
```

Lastly, the `resolve` property allows configuring how modules
should be resolved. This might include specifying alias for paths
(making imports cleaner) or extensions that should be processed.

Each of these properties and their sub-properties allows for
fine-grained control over the bundling process, enabling developers
to tailor the build process to the unique requirements of their
projects. Mastery over these configurations is essential for

exploiting Webpack's full capabilities to simplify and enhance your development workflow.

2.2   Understanding Entry and Context

In the domain of Webpack configurations, two fundamental concepts that play pivotal roles are the entry and context. These concepts serve as the starting points and environmental settings of the Webpack compilation process. Our aim here is to decode their functionalities, illustrate their use cases, and present configuration examples.   The understanding of entry and context is indispensable for tailoring the Webpack behavior to fit specific project needs.

Entry

The entry property signifies the inception point for Webpack. It instructs Webpack on which file or files should be used to commence the building process. This can be a single entry for smaller projects or multiple entries for larger applications that require separate bundle files.

A typical entry configuration is as follows:

```
1  module.exports = {
2    entry: './path/to/my/entry/file.js'
3  };
```

For applications necessitating multiple entry points, the configuration would adopt a slightly more complex structure:

```
1  module.exports = {
2    entry: {
3      app: './src/app.js',
4      admin: './src/admin.js'
5    }
6  };
```

In this scenario, Webpack generates two outputs, each originating from its respective entry point. This configuration is particularly useful for creating distinct bundles for different parts of an application, such as a public user interface and an admin panel.

Context

The `context` configuration sets the base directory for resolving the entry points. It is essentially the reference point or the environment from which your project runs. The significance of `context` becomes pronounced in scenarios where your project structure is not conventional, requiring a clear definition of the working directory for Webpack. If not explicitly set, `context` defaults to the current working directory.

Example of setting `context`:

```
1  module.exports = {
2    context: path.resolve(__dirname, 'src'),
3    entry: {
4      app: './app.js',
5      admin: './admin.js'
6    }
7  };
```

In this example, `context` is set to the `src` directory within the project. Webpack will now look for `app.js` and `admin.js` within the `src` directory. This configuration ensures that relative paths in the `entry` configuration are evaluated in relation to the specified `context`.

To sum up, `entry` and `context` are foundational to the configuration of Webpack, dictating the entry points for module bundling and setting the environment context, respectively. Proper utilization of these configurations paves the way for effective and efficient project builds, tailored specifically to the needs of the application.

2.3 Configuring Output: Filenames and Paths

The output property in Webpack's configuration is fundamental for defining how the compiled files are outputted – where they're saved and what they're named. Adjusting these settings lets you structure your output directory in a way that best suits your project's requirements.

To specify the output settings in your Webpack configuration, you will use the output object. This object can contain several properties, but the most crucial ones are path and filename.

Path: The path property defines the absolute path to the directory where the output files should be stored. It's worth noting that this path must be an absolute path, not relative. This requirement is to eliminate confusion and errors related to the file location. You can use Node.js's path module to assist in generating an absolute path.

```
1   const path = require('path');
2
3   module.exports = {
4     output: {
5       path: path.resolve(__dirname, 'dist'),
6     },
7   };
```

In the above example, __dirname is a Node.js global variable that gives the directory name of the current module. This, combined with path.resolve(), produces an absolute path to the dist directory where Webpack will place the output files.

Filename: The filename property specifies the name of the output file or files. For projects that output a single bundle, a static name can be used. However, for more complex setups producing multiple bundles, it's common to include placeholders (like [name] or [hash]) to ensure filenames are unique and identifiable.

```
1   module.exports = {
2     output: {
3       filename: 'bundle.js',
4     },
5   };
```

This configuration will result in the output file being named bundle.js. For multiple entry points, placeholders can be incorporated into the filename to generate distinctive names for each output bundle.

```
1  module.exports = {
2    output: {
3      filename: '[name].bundle.js',
4    },
5  };
```

Here, [name] is a placeholder that Webpack will replace with the name of each entry point. Thus, if you have entry points named app and vendor, the output filenames will be app.bundle.js and vendor.bundle.js respectively.

PublicPath: Another important property to consider is publicPath. This property specifies the public URL of the output directory when referenced in a browser. This is especially relevant for applications served from a domain or sub-directory. It ensures that assets are correctly referenced in HTML, CSS, and JavaScript.

```
1  module.exports = {
2    output: {
3      publicPath: '/assets/',
4    },
5  };
```

With publicPath set to '/assets/', Webpack will prepend '/assets/' to all asset URLs in the compiled output. As a result, if your application references an image, Webpack will adjust its path to include the publicPath, ensuring it loads correctly from its web-served location.

In summary, correctly configuring the output property in Webpack is crucial for controlling where and under what name your bundles are outputted. By adjusting the path, filename, and publicPath, you can fine-tune how Webpack outputs files to match the structure and requirements of your project.

2.4 Mastering Loaders: Test, Use, and Options

Webpack loaders play a crucial role in interpreting and transforming files before they are added to the bundle. Loaders allow Webpack to process more than just JavaScript files, enabling a wide array of file types such as CSS, HTML, and images to be treated as modules. This section elucidates the configuration of loaders, focusing on the test, use, and options properties, which are instrumental in defining how different types of files are handled during the build process.

Firstly, it's essential to understand the place of loaders in the Webpack configuration object. Loaders are defined within the module.rules array, each rule describing how to process a specific type of file. Let's begin with an illustrative example:

```
1  module.exports = {
2    module: {
3      rules: [
4        {
5          test: /\.txt$/,
6          use: 'raw-loader'
7        }
8      ]
9    }
10 };
```

In the above configuration, test is a regular expression that identifies which files should be processed by the loader. Here, any file ending in .txt will be matched. The use property specifies which loader should be applied to these files, in this case, raw-loader.

The power of loaders does not stop with simple file processing. Loaders can be chained to perform multiple transformations. They are executed in reverse order, starting from the last loader in the array to the first. This is important for understanding how to compose loader chains:

```
1  module.exports = {
2    module: {
3      rules: [
4        {
5          test: /\.scss$/,
6          use: [
```

44

```
 7          'style-loader',
 8          'css-loader',
 9          'sass-loader'
10        ]
11      }
12    ]
13  }
14 };
```

In this configuration, .scss files undergo three transformations. First, sass-loader converts SCSS into CSS. Next, css-loader interprets the CSS into a JavaScript module. Finally, style-loader injects the styles into the DOM.

The options property allows further customization of loaders' behavior. This property is an object where each key-value pair specifies options for the loader. Here is how you can use it with the css-loader to enable CSS modules:

```
 1 module.exports = {
 2   module: {
 3     rules: [
 4       {
 5         test: /\.css$/,
 6         use: [
 7           'style-loader',
 8           {
 9             loader: 'css-loader',
10             options: {
11               modules: true
12             }
13           }
14         ]
15       }
16     ]
17   }
18 };
```

This configuration modifies the behavior of the css-loader, enabling CSS modules, a technique to scope CSS class names locally by default, thus avoiding class name clashes.

To summarize, mastering loaders in Webpack requires understanding the test, use, and options properties. The test property allows you to specify which files should be processed. The use property defines which loaders and in what order should be applied. Lastly, the options property offers a way to customize the behavior of individual loaders, making it possible to fine-tune how files are processed based on project-specific requirements.

2.5   Incorporating Plugins into Your Build Process

Plugins are essential in extending Webpack's capabilities far beyond its default functionality. They allow developers to perform a wide range of tasks such as bundle optimization, asset management, and environmental variable injection. This section will guide through the process of selecting, configuring, and using various plugins within a Webpack build.

Plugins are applied in the configuration file through the `plugins` array. Each plugin is an instance of its constructor function, often requiring new keyword. The construction parameters allow customization of the plugin's behavior. Below is a simple example demonstrating how to include a plugin:

```
1   const HtmlWebpackPlugin = require('html-webpack-plugin');
2
3   module.exports = {
4     // Other configuration options...
5     plugins: [
6       new HtmlWebpackPlugin({
7         title: 'Webpack Demo',
8       }),
9     ],
10  };
```

This snippet exemplifies the incorporation of HtmlWebpackPlugin, a popular plugin for generating HTML files that automatically injects your bundle or bundles. Configuring it merely needs the title for the generated HTML file.

To further illustrate the breadth of operations possible with plugins, consider the following example that employs several widely used plugins:

```
1   const { CleanWebpackPlugin } = require('clean-webpack-plugin');
2   const MiniCssExtractPlugin = require('mini-css-extract-plugin');
3   const TerserJSPlugin = require('terser-webpack-plugin');
```

```
4    const OptimizeCSSAssetsPlugin = require('optimize-css-assets-webpack-plugin');
5
6    module.exports = {
7      // Previous configurations...
8      plugins: [
9        new CleanWebpackPlugin(),
10       new MiniCssExtractPlugin(),
11       new TerserJSPlugin({}),
12       new OptimizeCSSAssetsPlugin({})
13     ],
14   };
```

In this configuration, `CleanWebpackPlugin` is utilized to clean the /dist folder before each build, ensuring that only the used files are generated. `MiniCssExtractPlugin` extracts CSS into separate files, a practice that enhances cacheability and parallelism on modern browsers. `TerserJSPlugin` and `OptimizeCSSAssetsPlugin` are optimization plugins for minifying JavaScript and CSS files, respectively.

The efficiency of incorporating plugins can be dramatically increased by understanding their respective roles and integration points within the Webpack ecosystem. Notice the explicit use of the new keyword to instantiate each plugin, signaling to Webpack to prepare and utilize these plugins according to the provided configurations.

For complex projects, conditional loading of plugins might be necessary. This approach enables the inclusion of certain plugins only in specific environments, such as development or production. This can be achieved by constructing the plugins array dynamically based on the value of process.env.NODE_ENV or any other environment variable deemed relevant. The following is a simplified illustration:

```
1    const plugins = [
2      // Common Plugins...
3    ];
4
5    if(process.env.NODE_ENV === 'production') {
6      plugins.push(new TerserJSPlugin({}), new OptimizeCSSAssetsPlugin({}));
7    }
8
9    module.exports = {
10     // Other Webpack configurations...
11     plugins,
12   };
```

In this scenario, `TerserJSPlugin` and `OptimizeCSSAssetsPlugin` are only incorporated into the build process when it is run in a production environment, harnessing their capabilities for asset optimization without impacting the development build speed.

Finally, it is worthwhile to explore the extensive plugin ecosystem available in Webpack's community. Developers are encouraged to look for plugins that might solve specific problems or add desired functionality to their build process. Regularly reviewing the Webpack's official documentation and community resources can uncover new and improved ways to enhance your projects with plugins.

2.6   Resolving Modules: Configuration Tips

When configuring Webpack, one of the significant challenges developers encounter is managing the resolution of modules. Modules in Webpack are the building blocks of your application; they can be scripts, CSS, images, or any other assets. The way Webpack locates these modules when you import them in your code is through the resolve configuration. This part of the configuration is critical, as it directly affects the build time performance and the simplicity of the import statements in your project.

Let's delve into the key properties under the resolve configuration and how they can be effectively utilized to streamline your development process.

Extensions

The `extensions` array in the resolve configuration specifies the file extensions that Webpack will resolve. By default, Webpack attempts to resolve these extensions in order: `.js`, `.json`, `.wasm`. If your project uses other extensions frequently, such as `.jsx` or `.vue`, adding them to this list can simplify the import statements by omitting the extension.

```
1  resolve: {
2    extensions: ['.js', '.jsx', '.json']
3  }
```

Alias

To simplify deep import paths, the alias configuration can be used. An alias is a shorter name or a nickname for a module or path. This lets you avoid relative path hell (../../) by creating a more readable and maintainable codebase.

```
1  resolve: {
2    alias: {
3      Components: path.resolve(__dirname, 'src/components/'),
4      Images: path.resolve(__dirname, 'src/images/')
5    }
6  }
```

With the above configuration, instead of using relative paths, you can refer to a component or an image directly using Components/MyComponent or Images/logo.png.

Modules

The modules array tells Webpack where to look for modules. By default, Webpack will only search in the node_modules directory. If you have modules in other directories or you want to prioritize certain directories, you can modify this array. For example, you might want to add a lib folder at the root of your project or a vendor folder with third-party modules.

```
1  resolve: {
2    modules: [path.resolve(__dirname, 'src'), 'node_modules']
3  }
```

Resolve Plugins

Webpack also allows the use of plugins to customize the module resolution. For instance, the DirectoryNamedWebpackPlugin can make Webpack match directories' names with the file contained within, which is particularly useful for React projects where a file name matches its enclosing folder name.

```
1  const DirectoryNamedWebpackPlugin = require('directory-named-webpack-plugin');
2
3  resolve: {
4    plugins: [new DirectoryNamedWebpackPlugin(true)]
5  }
```

Main Fields

When importing a module from a package, Webpack decides which file to include based on the mainFields property. This property is an array of strings that specify the fields in package.json to look at, and in what order. For browser builds, this usually starts with "browser", then "module", and "main".

```
1  resolve: {
2    mainFields: ['browser', 'module', 'main']
3  }
```

To sum up, the resolve configuration in Webpack is a powerful feature that allows you to streamline module resolution, reduce code verbosity, and tailor the resolving logic to your project's specific needs. Leveraging extensions, aliases, module directories, plugins, and mainFields can significantly enhance your development experience and build process. Experiment with these settings in your webpack.config.js to find the most optimal configuration for your project.

2.7   Optimization Configuration: Splitting Chunks and Minimizing

Optimization configuration in Webpack is an essential toolset for improving the performance of a web application. Specifically, the splitting chunks and minimizing functions play pivotal roles in enhancing the application's load time and reducing the bundle size, which are critical for user experience and efficient resource utilization. This section will discuss these two optimization techniques in detail, including their configuration and application.

Splitting Chunks

Splitting chunks is a technique used to divide a larger bundle into smaller, more manageable chunks of files that can be loaded on demand or in parallel, improving page load times. This is particularly beneficial for applications with a significant amount of code or those using libraries and modules shared across multiple points.

Configuration

Webpack provides the `optimization.splitChunks` setting for configuring chunk splitting behavior. Below is an example of how to specify chunk splitting in the Webpack configuration file:

```
module.exports = {
  optimization: {
    splitChunks: {
      chunks: 'all',
      minSize: 20000,
      maxSize: 0,
      minChunks: 1,
      maxAsyncRequests: 30,
      maxInitialRequests: 30,
      automaticNameDelimiter: '~',
      enforceSizeThreshold: 50000,
      cacheGroups: {
        defaultVendors: {
          test: /[\\/]node_modules[\\/]/,
          priority: -10
        },
        default: {
          minChunks: 2,
          priority: -20,
          reuseExistingChunk: true
        }
      }
    }
  }
};
```

Explanation

In the above configuration, the `splitChunks` object contains several key properties that define how chunks should be split:

- `chunks:` `'all'` indicates that chunks are split for all types of chunks (asynchronous and non-asynchronous).

- `minSize` specifies the minimum size for a chunk to be generated.

- `maxAsyncRequests` and `maxInitialRequests` limit the number of simultaneous chunk requests.

- `cacheGroups` is an object that defines conditions for grouping modules into chunks. This setting allows the creation of a vendors chunk, containing modules from the `node_modules` directory, separated from the application code.

Minimizing

Minimization is the process of reducing the bundle size by removing unnecessary spaces, comments, and modifications in the code without altering its functionality. Webpack uses TerserPlugin, a plugin for JavaScript optimization, for this purpose.

Configuration

To enable minimizing in Webpack, the `optimization.minimize` property is set to true, and `optimization.minimizer` is used to add the TerserPlugin as shown below:

```
1   const TerserPlugin = require('terser-webpack-plugin');
2
3   module.exports = {
4     optimization: {
5       minimize: true,
6       minimizer: [
7         new TerserPlugin({
8           terserOptions: {
9             compress: {
```

```
10        drop_console: true,
11       },
12      },
13     }),
14    ],
15   },
16 };
```

Explanation

In this configuration, `minimize: true` activates the minimization process. The `minimizer` array allows specifying custom minimization plugins and their configurations. `TerserPlugin` is configured to remove console logs from the output bundle through `compress: {drop_console: true}`, contributing to a smaller bundle size.

Understanding and implementing optimization configuration, specifically splitting chunks and minimizing, are vital steps in Webpack configuration. By applying these techniques, developers can significantly increase their application's performance and provide a better end-user experience.

```
Execution successfully finished. Your Webpack configuration is now optimized.
```

2.8 Environment Configurations: Development, Production, and Custom

Webpack's flexibility allows developers to configure their projects for different environments. This ensures that the development environment is optimized for speed and debugging, while the production environment focuses on reducing file sizes, improving load times, and enhancing the overall user experience. Custom environments can also be defined for specific use cases. This section explains how to differentiate these configurations effectively.

Development Configuration

In development mode, source maps and local servers are typically prioritized to enhance the debugging process. Setting up a development configuration in Webpack involves several key adjustments:

- Enabling source maps by setting the `devtool` property to a value like `'inline-source-map'`. This allows errors to be traced back to the original source code instead of the bundled code.

- Using the `webpack-dev-server` to serve the application. This tool provides live reloading, which automatically refreshes the browser upon file changes.

- Configuring Hot Module Replacement (HMR) to update modules in the browser without requiring a full refresh.

These features can be configured in the Webpack configuration file as follows:

```
1  module.exports = {
2     mode: 'development',
3     devtool: 'inline-source-map',
4     devServer: {
5        contentBase: './dist',
6        hot: true
7     },
8     // Additional configuration...
9  };
```

Production Configuration

The production environment focuses on optimization techniques to minimize the size of the bundle and ensure the application runs efficiently for the end user. This involves:

- Minimizing CSS and JavaScript files using plugins like `MiniCssExtractPlugin` and `TerserWebpackPlugin`.

- Splitting code to facilitate quicker loading times by leveraging Webpack's `splitChunks` settings.

- Setting the mode property to `'production'` which automatically enables several optimization features.

A basic production configuration example is shown below:

```
1  const MiniCssExtractPlugin = require('mini-css-extract-plugin');
2  const TerserJSPlugin = require('terser-webpack-plugin');
3  const OptimizeCSSAssetsPlugin = require('optimize-css-assets-webpack-
      plugin');
4
5  module.exports = {
6      mode: 'production',
7      optimization: {
8          minimizer: [new TerserJSPlugin({}), new OptimizeCSSAssetsPlugin
              ({})],
9      },
10     plugins: [
11         new MiniCssExtractPlugin({
12             filename: '[name].[contenthash].css',
13         }),
14     ],
15     // Additional configuration...
16 };
```

Custom Environment Configuration

In some scenarios, neither standard development nor production configurations fully meet the project's needs. It might be necessary to create a custom environment, such as a testing environment that closely mirrors production but includes additional logging and debugging information.

Webpack allows for the creation of custom environment configurations through the use of the --env command line argument, which passes environment variables to the configuration file. This enables dynamic configuration adjustments based on the specified environment.

To implement a custom environment configuration, modify the Web-

pack configuration to accept an environment parameter and conditionally apply settings as shown:

```
1  module.exports = env => {
2     return {
3        mode: env.production ? 'production' : 'development',
4        // Further conditional configuration...
5     };
6  };
```

This approach facilitates fine-grained control over the build process,
allowing developers to tailor the setup to precisely match the requirements of any given environment.

In wrapping up the discussion on environment configurations, it's
clear that Webpack provides a robust set of tools for fine-tuning the
build process to suit different deployment scenarios. By leveraging
environment-specific configurations, developers can ensure that
their applications are optimized across all stages of development
and deployment.

2.9   Using Webpack with TypeScript

TypeScript offers static typing capabilities to JavaScript, enhancing
code reliability and maintainability in large-scale applications. Integrating TypeScript with Webpack requires specific configurations to
ensure both tools function synergistically. This section will outline
the steps to set up Webpack to work with TypeScript projects, highlighting essential loaders and plugins, and providing practical examples.

First, TypeScript needs to be transpiled into JavaScript, as Webpack
does not natively understand TypeScript. This is achieved by using
the 'ts-loader' or 'babel-loader'. The choice between these loaders depends on specific project requirements, including the need for Babel
presets or plugins that may not be supported by TypeScript alone.

- To use 'ts-loader', first install TypeScript and the loader itself
  via npm:

```
1   npm install --save-dev typescript ts-loader
```

- For projects that already use Babel or require Babel's additional features, 'babel-loader' can be configured to work with Type-Script:

```
1   npm install --save-dev @babel/core @babel/preset-typescript babel-loader
```

After installing the necessary loader, the next step is to configure Webpack to use it. This involves modifying the Webpack configuration file, usually named 'webpack.config.js'.

```
1   module.exports = {
2     entry: './src/index.ts',
3     module: {
4       rules: [
5         {
6           test: /\.tsx?$/,
7           use: 'ts-loader',
8           exclude: /node_modules/,
9         },
10      ],
11    },
12    resolve: {
13      extensions: ['.tsx', '.ts', '.js'],
14    },
15  };
```

In this configuration, 'entry' points to the main entry file of the application, which, for a TypeScript project, typically ends in '.ts' or '.tsx' if using JSX. The 'rules' section includes a rule object that specifies 'ts-loader' to process files matching the '.ts' or '.tsx' extension, excluding any files in 'node_modules'. The 'resolve' section adds '.ts' and '.tsx' as recognizable extensions, allowing imports without needing to specify the extension.

TypeScript itself also requires configuration via a 'tsconfig.json' file. A simple 'tsconfig.json' might look as follows:

```
1   {
2     "compilerOptions": {
3       "outDir": "./dist/",
4       "noImplicitAny": true,
5       "module": "es6",
6       "target": "es5",
7       "jsx": "react",
```

```
 8        "allowJs": true
 9      },
10      "include": [
11        "./src/**/*"
12      ]
13    }
```

This configuration specifies various compiler options:

- 'outDir' determines where the transpiled JavaScript files will be placed. - 'noImplicitAny' prevents TypeScript from inferring 'any' types, enforcing more strict type checking. - 'module' and 'target' set the module system and JavaScript version for the output files. - 'jsx' is set to 'react' for projects using React with JSX syntax. - 'allowJs' allows JavaScript files to be compiled along with TypeScript.

For projects combining JavaScript and TypeScript, or when leveraging newer ECMAScript features not yet supported by the environment, integrating Webpack and TypeScript becomes crucial. By correctly setting up the development environment as described, developers can enjoy the benefits of TypeScript's type system while maintaining the flexibility and powerful features of Webpack.

2.10   Conditional Loading and Feature Flags

Conditional loading and the use of feature flags are advanced techniques that can substantially enhance the flexibility and maintainability of a Webpack bundle.   These strategies allow developers to include or exclude modules and code paths based on specific conditions, such as the target environment (development, testing, production) or feature availability.   This section elucidates the implementation of conditional loading and feature flags within a Webpack configuration, offering guidance and exemplary code snippets.

First, it's pivotal to understand the premise of conditional loading in Webpack. This can be accomplished by leveraging Webpack's built-in support for environment variables and the DefinePlugin, which

allows you to create global constants which can be configured at compile time.

```
// webpack.config.js
const webpack = require('webpack');

module.exports = (env) => {
  return {
    plugins: [
      new webpack.DefinePlugin({
        'process.env.FEATURE_FLAG': JSON.stringify(env.FEATURE_FLAG)
      })
    ]
  };
};
```

In the above example, env.FEATURE_FLAG is an environment variable
passed through the build script. This variable can toggle the visibility
of specific features or code paths in your application.

Next, let's discuss the practical application within your code. You
can utilize the defined feature flags to conditionally require modules
or wrap chunks of your code.

```
if (process.env.FEATURE_FLAG === 'true') {
  require('./feature-module');
}
```

The use of require() in this manner allows for code to be
conditionally   included   based   on   the   value   of
process.env.FEATURE_FLAG, which is determined at build time.
This technique can be employed to optimize your application,
ensuring that only necessary code is included and initialized.

Furthermore, feature flags can be utilized to implement A/B testing
or rolling out new features gradually, enhancing the user experience
while providing valuable feedback on feature adoption and usage.

In order to further refine the handling of conditional loading, it's rec-
ommendable to structure your application to support dynamic imports. Webpack supports the import() syntax, which allows you to
dynamically import modules only when they're needed, known as
code-splitting.

```
if (process.env.FEATURE_FLAG === 'true') {
  import('./feature-module')
    .then(featureModule => {
```

```
4        // Use the dynamically imported module
5      })
6      .catch(error => {
7        // Handle errors, such as feature not supported
8      });
9    }
```

This method enhances the performance of your application by reducing the initial load time, as features are loaded on-demand rather than at the initial boot time.

To summarize, effectively leveraging conditional loading and feature flags in your Webpack configuration can vastly improve both the development experience and the end-user experience by optimizing loading times, enabling gradual feature rollout, and facilitating A/B testing. These techniques, coupled with Webpack's robust configuration options and support for dynamic imports, empower developers to build highly efficient, scalable, and maintainable web applications.

2.11   Analyzing Build: Tools and Techniques

Analyzing the build process is a critical step in optimizing the performance and efficiency of your web applications. This section will discuss the various tools and techniques available for analyzing Webpack builds, providing insights into how you can identify bottlenecks, optimize asset sizes, and improve the overall build time.

Webpack Bundle Analyzer

One of the most popular tools for analyzing Webpack bundles is the `Webpack Bundle Analyzer`. This plugin provides a visual representation of the size of your output files, allowing you to easily identify which modules are contributing most to the bundle size.

To integrate `Webpack Bundle Analyzer` into your build process, you first need to install it via npm or yarn:

```
1  npm install --save-dev webpack-bundle-analyzer
```

or

```
1  yarn add --dev webpack-bundle-analyzer
```

Once installed, you can add it to your Webpack configuration file as follows:

```
1  const BundleAnalyzerPlugin = require('webpack-bundle-analyzer').
      BundleAnalyzerPlugin;
2
3  module.exports = {
4    // Your existing configuration
5    plugins: [
6      new BundleAnalyzerPlugin()
7    ]
8  };
```

When you run your build, the Webpack Bundle Analyzer will open up a web page in your default browser, displaying a treemap visualization of your bundle. Each module is represented as a box, with sizes proportional to the module's size in the bundle.

Speed Measure Plugin

While the Webpack Bundle Analyzer helps in identifying large modules, the Speed Measure Plugin (SMP) assists in pinpointing slow parts of your build process. SMP measures the speed of various Webpack plugins and loaders, giving you a detailed breakdown of build times.

To use SMP, first install it:

```
1  npm install --save-dev speed-measure-webpack-plugin
```

Then, wrap your Webpack configuration with SMP as shown:

```
1  const SpeedMeasurePlugin = require("speed-measure-webpack-plugin");
2  const smp = new SpeedMeasurePlugin();
3
4  const webpackConfig = {
5    // Your Webpack configuration
6  };
7
```

```
8   module.exports = smp.wrap(webpackConfig);
```

After integrating SMP and running your build, you'll receive a detailed report in your console, showing how long each plugin and loader took to execute.   This information is invaluable for identifying performance bottlenecks in your build process.

Custom Scripts

Beyond existing tools, custom scripts can be written to analyze specific aspects of your build. For instance, you can create a script to monitor the size of your assets over time, alerting you when a threshold is exceeded.

A basic Node.js script to log the sizes of your output files might look like this:

```
1   const fs = require('fs');
2   const path = require('path');
3
4   const outputPath = path.join(__dirname, 'dist');
5
6   fs.readdir(outputPath, (err, files) => {
7     files.forEach(file => {
8       const filePath = path.join(outputPath, file);
9       fs.stat(filePath, (err, stats) => {
10        console.log(`${file}: ${stats.size} bytes`);
11      });
12    });
13  });
```

This script reads all files in the dist directory and logs their sizes in bytes. Custom scripts like this can be adapted and extended to meet the specific needs of your project.

By leveraging tools like the Webpack Bundle Analyzer and the Speed Measure Plugin, along with custom scripts tailored to your specific requirements, you can gain deep insights into your Webpack build process. This analysis enables you to make informed decisions on how to optimize your configurations, leading to faster build times and more efficient application delivery.

2.12 Best Practices in Webpack Configuration

Adopting best practices in Webpack configuration not only stream-lines development work but also optimizes the performance of the application. As we move through the various aspects of these practices, the focus will be on ensuring efficiency, maintainability, and scalability of the Webpack setup.

Modularize the Configuration File: Splitting the Webpack configuration into multiple files can greatly improve readability and maintainability, especially for large-scale projects. Consider dividing the configuration into separate files for development, production, and common configurations. This can be achieved by using tools such as 'webpack-merge' to combine the configurations appropriately based on the build environment.

```
const { merge } = require('webpack-merge');
const commonConfig = require('./webpack.common.js');
const productionConfig = require('./webpack.prod.js');

module.exports = (env) => {
   switch(env.NODE_ENV) {
      case 'production':
         return merge(commonConfig, productionConfig);
      default:
         return commonConfig;
   }
};
```

Leverage Caching for Better Performance: Webpack allows the use of caching to speed up build times. Utilizing 'cache-loader' or en-abling caching in loaders that support it can make subsequent builds faster by caching the results of expensive loader transformations.

```
module.exports = {
   module: {
      rules: [
         {
            test: /\.js$/,
            use: ['cache-loader', 'babel-loader'],
         },
      ],
   },
};
```

Optimize Your Build with Tree Shaking: Tree shaking is a form of dead code elimination. By specifying the 'sideEffects' flag in your package.json or using ES modules, you help Webpack to identify and eliminate unused modules, resulting in a smaller bundle size.

```
"sideEffects": false
```

Code Splitting for Lazier Loading: Splitting code into various bundles which can then be loaded on demand or in parallel can significantly improve performance. Use import() syntax for dynamic imports, splitting off code paths that aren't essential for the initial load of your application.

```
1   const MainComponent = React.lazy(() => import('./MainComponent'));
```

Use Hashes in Output Filenames for Cache Busting: Including content-specific hashes in file names enables long-term caching, as browsers can cache these files without risk of cache invalidation when file contents change.

```
1   output: {
2       filename: '[name].[chunkhash].js'
3   }
```

Environment-Specific   Configurations: Differentiating configurations based on environment (development, testing, production) is crucial for optimizing performance and debugging capabilities. Use environment variables to toggle between different configurations smoothly.

Incorporate Plugins Wisely: While Webpack plugins can add powerful functionalities to your build, it's important to evaluate the necessity and performance impact of each plugin. Aim to use plugins that significantly benefit your development workflow or optimization requirements.

- Use HtmlWebpackPlugin to generate HTML files that include your bundles.

- Employ MiniCssExtractPlugin for extracting CSS into separate files.

- Leverage `CleanWebpackPlugin` for cleaning up the `/dist` folder before each build.

Analyze and Monitor Bundle Size: Regularly auditing your bundle size with Webpack's built-in analytics tools or third-party plugins can reveal opportunities for optimization, helping to keep your application lean and performant.

```
1  module.exports = {
2      plugins: [
3          new BundleAnalyzerPlugin()
4      ]
5  }
```

Documentation and Comments: Maintaining up-to-date documentation and commenting within your Webpack configuration files is essential for future maintenance, especially in team environments. This practice ensures that configurations are accessible and understandable to all team members.

Following these best practices in Webpack configuration not only streamlines the development process but also significantly impacts the performance and scalability of your application. By adopting a thoughtful approach to configuration, developers can leverage the full power of Webpack in their projects.

Chapter 3

Working with Loaders

Loaders play a critical role in Webpack, allowing the bundler to process and convert files of various types before they are added to the dependency graph. This chapter focuses on the utilization of loaders to manage and transform CSS, images, and JavaScript, among other assets. It elucidates the principles of configuring loaders, details the usage of popular loaders like css-loader, file-loader, and babel-loader, and offers guidance on creating custom loaders for specific needs. Through practical examples, readers will learn how to integrate and fine-tune loaders to efficiently handle project assets within their Webpack configuration.

3.1 Understanding Loaders in Webpack

Loaders in Webpack are fundamentally transformative functions that allow the processing of files imported or loaded into your application before they are added to the dependency graph. Typically, Webpack only understands JavaScript and JSON files natively. However, Webpack's functionality can be extended to process other types of files through the use of loaders. The primary responsibility of loaders is to transform these files into modules as they are added to your application's dependency graph.

A loader in Webpack can convert files from a different format into JavaScript, or load inline images as data URLs. Essentially, loaders allow you to preprocess files as you import or "load" them. Beyond mere file transformation, loaders have the capability to chain through multiple steps, offering a powerful means to configure the preprocessing steps in your application pipeline.

To utilize loaders in Webpack, two properties within your Webpack configuration object need to be configured: module.rules and module.loaders. It is important to note that module.loaders is used in Webpack 1.x, though it has been deprecated in favor of module.rules in later versions. This section will focus on the syntax and configuration as it applies to module.rules.

```
module: {
  rules: [
    {test: /\.css$/, use: 'css-loader'}
  ]
}
```

In the above example, the configuration tells Webpack to use the css-loader for all files ending in .css. The test property in the rule object requires a regular expression to match the file types that the loader should be applied to. The use property then specifies which loader to use for these files.

Loaders can be applied in two ways: pre-processing or inline. Pre-processing loaders are defined in the Webpack configuration and apply to the project on a global scope. Inline loaders can be specified within the import statement of a file, offering more granular control over loader application without necessitating global configuration changes.

```
1   import Styles from 'style-loader!css-loader?modules!./styles.css';
```

In the above example, the style-loader and css-loader are applied inline to styles.css file. The css-loader processes the CSS file, and the style-loader then injects the styles into the DOM. The query parameters (modules) in the css-loader demonstrate how to pass options to loaders, enabling CSS modules in this instance.

It is essential to understand the order of execution when using multiple loaders, as they are applied from right to left (or bottom to top when configured as an array of objects). Therefore, in the chain of loaders, the last loader is applied first.

To summarize, loaders in Webpack are indispensable for handling a wide array of file types and preprocessing tasks. Proper configuration and application of loaders empower developers to seamlessly integrate various assets into their applications, enhancing the modular architecture and maintainability of the project. Understanding loaders' syntax, application scopes, and execution order is critical in leveraging their full potential within your Webpack configuration.

3.2 Setting Up CSS Loaders for Style Management

Setting up CSS loaders in Webpack is an essential process for incorporating CSS into your project. This section elucidates the configuration of CSS loaders, specifically focusing on `style-loader` and `css-loader`. The integration of these loaders allows Webpack to process CSS files, inject styles into the DOM, and bundle them along with your JavaScript files.

To commence, install the required loaders via npm:

```
1  npm install --save-dev style-loader css-loader
```

Once installed, you must include these loaders in your Webpack configuration file. Ensure that your `webpack.config.js` file is configured to utilize these loaders for handling `.css` files. This is accomplished by adding a module rule as follows:

```
1  module.exports = {
2    // ...
3    module: {
4      rules: [
5        {
6          test: /\.css$/i,
7          use: ['style-loader', 'css-loader'],
```

```
 8        },
 9      ],
10    },
11    // ...
12  };
```

The configuration specifies a rule that utilizes a regular expression to match files ending with .css. For those files, it applies two loaders: css-loader and style-loader. The css-loader interprets '@import' and 'url()' like import/require() and will resolve them, while the style-loader injects the resulting CSS into the DOM by adding a <style> tag.

Important Note: Loaders in Webpack are evaluated from right to left (or bottom to top). Therefore, in the configuration provided above, css-loader processes the CSS file first, followed by style-loader which takes the output from css-loader and adds it to the DOM.

For projects where CSS needs to be bundled separately rather than injected into the DOM, an alternative setup involving the MiniCssExtractPlugin instead of style-loader may be preferable. This approach is particularly beneficial for production environments where performance and caching of CSS files are important considerations. The configuration adjustment for utilizing MiniCssExtractPlugin is as follows:

```
 1  const MiniCssExtractPlugin = require('mini-css-extract-plugin');
 2
 3  module.exports = {
 4    // ...
 5    module: {
 6      rules: [
 7        {
 8          test: /\.css$/,
 9          use: [MiniCssExtractPlugin.loader, 'css-loader'],
10        },
11      ],
12    },
13    plugins: [new MiniCssExtractPlugin()],
14    // ...
15  };
```

By substituting style-loader with MiniCssExtractPlugin.loader, the CSS is instead extracted into its own file, typically named style.css, that gets linked in the HTML head.

Practical Example: If we have a `styles.css` file containing simple CSS rules, we can import this CSS file into our JavaScript entry point, and Webpack will process it according to the loaders specified in the configuration.

```
1   import './styles.css';
```

The resulting behavior, whether injecting styles directly into the DOM or outputting a separate CSS file, depends entirely on the loaders and configuration specified in the `webpack.config.js` file.

Lastly, it's worth mentioning some common issues encountered when setting up CSS loaders. Ensure that the path to your CSS files is correct and that your Webpack configuration properly matches the file extension patterns. Misconfiguration can lead to styles not being applied as expected.

To summarize, the setup of CSS loaders in Webpack facilitates the inclusion and management of styles within your project. Proper configuration and understanding of `style-loader` and `css-loader` will enable efficient style management throughout the development process.

3.3 Handling Images and Fonts with File Loader

File Loader is a powerful utility in Webpack's arsenal for managing static assets like images and fonts. The core functionality is straightforward: it instructs Webpack to emit the required object as a file and to return its public URL.

To begin integrating File Loader for handling image and font files, the first step is installation. Include File Loader in your project by executing the command in your terminal:

```
1   npm install --save-dev file-loader
```

After the installation, the next phase involves the configuration of Webpack to use File Loader. This is achieved by adding a rule in the

Webpack configuration file, typically named `webpack.config.js`.
The rule specifies that File Loader should process files matching
certain conditions—usually file types identified by their extensions.

```
1   module.exports = {
2      module: {
3         rules: [
4            {
5               test: /\.(png|svg|jpg|jpeg|gif)$/i,
6               use: [
7                  {
8                     loader: 'file-loader',
9                     options: {
10                        outputPath: 'images',
11                     },
12                  },
13               ],
14            },
15            {
16               test: /\.(woff|woff2|eot|ttf|otf)$/i,
17               use: [
18                  {
19                     loader: 'file-loader',
20                     options: {
21                        outputPath: 'fonts',
22                     },
23                  },
24               ],
25            },
26         ],
27      },
28   };
```

In this configuration, two rules are defined under the `rules` array.
The first rule targets image files—identified by their extensions
(.png, .svg, .jpg, .jpeg, .gif)—and applies `file-loader` to them. The
second rule deals with font files, including .woff, .woff2, .eot, .ttf,
and .otf extensions. For both rules, `file-loader` is configured with
an `outputPath` option, specifying where the output files should be
stored relative to the output directory defined in the Webpack
configuration.

By using the `outputPath` option, it becomes possible to organize
compiled files into directories, thus maintaining a clean structure in
the output destination. This organization is particularly beneficial
for projects with a large number of assets.

Once configured, Webpack, in conjunction with File Loader,

automates the process of moving the source image and font files from their original locations to the output directory specified in the Webpack configuration. Furthermore, File Loader transforms the URLs within the code to reflect the path of the output files, ensuring that these static assets are correctly referenced and can be loaded by the client's browser.

Consider the scenario where an image file named `logo.png` is imported into a JavaScript module:

```
import logo from './logo.png';
```

Webpack processes this import statement, and File Loader handles the `logo.png` file. If the `outputPath` option is set to `'images'`, File Loader relocates `logo.png` to the `images` directory within the output destination. Moreover, the import statement's result, stored in the variable `logo`, becomes the URL string pointing to the output location of `logo.png`.

By effectively processing and managing static assets, File Loader enhances the capability to serve images and fonts in a Webpack-bundled application. This convenience underscores the importance of correctly configuring loaders in the Webpack ecosystem, enabling developers to focus more on development and less on manual asset management.

3.4   Transpiling JavaScript with Babel Loader

Transpiling JavaScript code is essential in ensuring that modern JavaScript features can be used while maintaining compatibility with older browsers. This is where Babel, a JavaScript compiler, comes into play. It allows developers to write code using the latest JavaScript syntax without worrying about support in older environments. To integrate Babel into a Webpack build process, the `babel-loader` is used. This section will cover the process of setting up and configuring the `babel-loader` within a Webpack configuration to transpile JavaScript files.

Installing Babel Loader and Babel Core

To begin, you must install both `babel-loader` and `@babel/core` as development dependencies. The `@babel/core` package is the core compiler for Babel, while `babel-loader` connects Babel with Webpack. This installation can be done using the following npm command:

```
1   npm install --save-dev babel-loader @babel/core
```

Babel Configuration File

Before proceeding to configure the `babel-loader` in your Webpack configuration, it is advisable to set up a Babel configuration file named `.babelrc`. This JSON-formatted file will specify the presets and plugins needed to transpile your JavaScript code.

.babelrc Configuration File

```
1   {
2     "presets": ["@babel/preset-env"]
3   }
```

Here, `@babel/preset-env` is a smart preset that allows you to use the latest JavaScript without needing to micromanage which syntax transforms are needed by your target environment(s).

Configuring Webpack to Use Babel Loader

With Babel installed and configured, the next step is to modify your Webpack configuration to use the `babel-loader` for JavaScript files. This is accomplished within the `module.rules` array in the `webpack.config.js` file.

```
1   module.exports = {
2     module: {
3       rules: [
4         {
5           test: /\.js$/,
6           exclude: /node_modules/,
```

```
 7          use: {
 8            loader: "babel-loader",
 9            options: {
10              presets: ["@babel/preset-env"]
11            }
12          }
13        }
14      ]
15    }
16  };
```

Webpack configuration using babel-loader

In this configuration, `module.rules` is used to define a set of rules for the types of files to be processed. Each rule can specify:

- A `test` property to identify which files should be transformed.

- An `exclude` property to filter out files or directories.

- A `use` property that specifies which loader to use for the transformation. Here, the `babel-loader` is used along with the `@babel/preset-env` preset.

Code Example

To demonstrate the effectiveness of `babel-loader`, consider this ES6 code snippet:

```
1  const greet = () => console.log("Hello, Webpack and Babel!");
2  greet();
```

Sample ES6 JavaScript code

After processing with Webpack and Babel, the output would not contain ES6 arrow functions, making the code compatible with older browsers. The transformation result might look like this:

```
"use strict";
var greet = function greet() {
  console.log("Hello, Webpack and Babel!");
};
greet();
```

75

This example illustrates how `babel-loader` transforms ES6 syntax into a form that can be understood by a wider range of browsers.

Additional Considerations

While the setup shown here is sufficient for basic JavaScript transpilation, Babel's functionality can be extended further through the use of additional plugins and presets. These allow for a broader range of JavaScript features and proposals to be used safely. Moreover, considering the evolving landscape of JavaScript, keeping Babel's dependencies up to date is crucial for taking advantage of the latest language improvements and ensuring compatibility.

Integrating `babel-loader` into your Webpack configuration offers a streamlined workflow for writing modern JavaScript that is both efficient and backward compatible. Through proper setup and occasional maintenance, developers can leverage the full power of the latest JavaScript features without compromising on compatibility.

3.5   Using the Sass Loader for SCSS Files

Loaders in Webpack are pivotal for handling various types of files, and for CSS preprocessing, the Sass loader plays an indispensable role. This loader enables the processing of SCSS (Sassy CSS) files into standard CSS that browsers can understand. In this section, we will discuss how to set up and integrate the Sass loader into your Webpack configuration.

Firstly, it's imperative to install the necessary npm packages. For the Sass loader to work, you need 'sass-loader', 'sass' itself (as the 'sass-loader' requires it as a peer dependency), and 'css-loader' to convert the resulting CSS into JavaScript. Additionally, 'style-loader' might be necessary to inject the CSS into the DOM. The installation command is as follows:

```
1   npm install sass-loader sass css-loader style-loader --save-dev
```

Once installed, configuration within your 'webpack.config.js' is required. The loaders work by chaining, processing from the last to the first. Here is an example configuration for integrating Sass loader:

```
module.exports = {
  module: {
    rules: [
      {
        test: /\.scss$/,
        use: [
          'style-loader', // 3. Inject styles into DOM
          'css-loader', // 2. Turns css into commonjs
          'sass-loader' // 1. Turns sass into css
        ]
      }
    ]
  }
};
```

In the configuration above, when a '.scss' file is encountered in the project, the Webpack processes it using the loaders in the specified order:

- The 'sass-loader' converts SCSS to CSS.

- The 'css-loader' takes the resulting CSS and converts it into a CommonJS module.

- Finally, the 'style-loader' injects the CSS into the DOM.

It's crucial to understand each loader's role in this chain for efficient debugging and configuration updates. The order is paramount as reversing it may lead to build errors or unexpected behavior.

For more elaborate projects, you might need to extract the CSS from your JavaScript files to create separate CSS files, which is achievable with the 'MiniCssExtractPlugin'. This can lead to better caching and page load performance.

```
const MiniCssExtractPlugin = require('mini-css-extract-plugin');

module.exports = {
```

```
4    module: {
5      rules: [
6        {
7          test: /\.scss$/,
8          use: [
9            MiniCssExtractPlugin.loader, // Instead of style-loader
10           'css-loader',
11           'sass-loader'
12         ]
13       }
14     ]
15   },
16   plugins: [
17     new MiniCssExtractPlugin({
18       filename: '[name].css',
19       chunkFilename: '[id].css',
20     }),
21   ],
22 };
```

In this setup, the 'MiniCssExtractPlugin.loader' replaces the 'style-loader', directing Webpack to bundle the processed CSS into separate files rather than injecting them into the DOM. This configuration is particularly useful for production environments.

Throughout this section, nuances of integrating and configuring the Sass loader within a Webpack setup were dissected elaborately. Adhering to these instructions will enable efficient handling and transformation of SCSS files in your projects, paving the way for more organized and manageable stylesheets.

3.6 Managing HTML Files with HTML Loader

Managing HTML files within a Webpack setup involves a nuanced approach, facilitated primarily by the html-loader. The utility of this loader lies in its ability to process HTML files, interpreting any embeddable assets such as images or fonts referenced within them, and returning a valid module that can be integrated into the Webpack bundle. This process not only optimizes asset management but also enhances the efficiency of deploying HTML-centric projects.

To commence integrating the html-loader into a Webpack configuration, it's imperative to first install the loader via the npm package manager. This can be achieved by executing the following command in the terminal:

```
npm install --save-dev html-loader
```

Following installation, the html-loader must be appropriately configured within the Webpack configuration file, typically named webpack.config.js. Configuration involves adding a rule object to the module's rules array, specifying the test and use properties to dictate the handling of '.html' files, as shown below:

```
module.exports = {
  module: {
    rules: [
      {
        test: /\.html$/,
        use: [
          {
            loader: 'html-loader',
            options: { minimize: true }
          }
        ]
      }
    ]
  }
};
```

In this configuration, the test property utilizes a regular expression to target files ending with the '.html' extension. The use property then specifies the html-loader, with an options object that includes a minimize property set to true. This option instructs the loader to minimize the HTML files, removing unnecessary whitespaces and comments, thus optimizing the output for production environments.

Handling images and other assets embedded within HTML files necessitates additional considerations. Specifically, when an img tag is encountered in an HTML file, the html-loader processes the image's source attribute (src), treating it as a module request. This behavior ensures that referenced images are incorporated into the Webpack bundle and paths are correctly resolved. Consequently, to manage these assets effectively, combining the html-loader with loaders such as `file-loader` or `url-loader` becomes essential, as demonstrated in the following configuration snippet:

```
1   {
2     test: /\.(png|svg|jpg|jpeg|gif)$/,
3     use: [
4       'file-loader',
5     ]
6   }
```

Implementing the `html-loader` extends beyond mere inclusion and configuration within the Webpack setup. It underscores a strategic approach to handling and optimizing HTML files and their associated assets, thereby streamlining the development and deployment process of web applications.

Addressing potential issues, one common challenge involves ensuring that all asset URLs within HTML files are correctly interpreted and processed. This may require additional configuration or the use of plugins to guarantee accurate path resolution and asset inclusion within the final bundle.

The `html-loader` plays a pivotal role in managing HTML files within a Webpack environment, facilitating the integration, optimization, and proper handling of HTML and its embeddable assets. Through comprehensive configuration and mindful consideration of asset management strategies, developers can harness the full potential of this loader to streamline their Webpack-based projects.

3.7   Optimizing   Performance   with   URL Loader

In this section, we will discuss the URL loader, a crucial element in the optimization of application performance. The URL loader works by converting files into base64 URIs, allowing them to be inlined in your code, which can significantly reduce the number of requests a browser makes to the server. This is particularly beneficial for small files, such as icons or small images, which can be loaded faster when

embedded directly into the code rather than fetched as separate resources.

First, it is important to understand that the Webpack configuration
must be correctly set up to include the URL loader. Here is an example of how to configure a Webpack module rule for using the URL
loader for image files:

```
 1  module.exports = {
 2    module: {
 3      rules: [
 4        {
 5          test: /\.(png|svg|jpg|jpeg|gif)$/i,
 6          use: [
 7            {
 8              loader: 'url-loader',
 9              options: {
10                limit: 8192,
11              },
12            },
13          ],
14        },
15      ],
16    },
17  };
```

In the configuration above, the `test` property is a RegExp that
matches the file extensions for most common image types. The
`loader` specifies the use of the url-loader. The `options` object
contains a `limit` field, which is pivotal in deciding whether a file
will be inlined or not. The value of `limit` is in bytes; in this case,
8192 bytes or 8 kilobytes. Files smaller than this limit will be
transformed into base64 URIs and inlined. Files larger will be
processed with file-loader, which must be installed alongside
url-loader.

To further illustrate the behavior of the URL loader, consider the following example:

```
 1  import smallImage from './small-image.png';
```

After processing with Webpack, assuming `small-image.png` is under the limit:

```
console.log(smallImage);
// Output will be a base64 URI
```

When the image is small enough to be inlined, the output logged to the console will be a base64 URI, which represents the binary content of the image encoded in base64. This URI can be used directly in image sources in your HTML or CSS, effectively eliminating the HTTP request that would otherwise be needed to load the image.

The URL loader plays a significant role in improving the performance of web applications by reducing the number of resource requests. This is achieved through the inline encoding of smaller files, which consequently decreases load times and enhances the overall user experience. When incorporating the URL loader into your Webpack configuration, it is crucial to carefully consider the limit option to balance between the performance benefits of inlining and the potential cost of increased bundle size.

3.8 Linting Code with ESLint Loader

Linting is a method of static code analysis to identify problematic patterns or code that doesn't adhere to certain style guidelines. Regarding JavaScript, ESLint is a powerful and widely-used tool for this purpose. Incorporating ESLint into a Webpack project can significantly improve code quality and maintainability. This section discusses the integration of ESLint Loader into a Webpack configuration, enabling ESLint to run automatically during the build process, thus ensuring that all JavaScript code conforms to defined coding standards before it's bundled.

First, it is essential to install ESLint and ESLint Loader into your project. This can be achieved through npm, the Node package manager. The following command installs both as development dependencies, ensuring they are only used during the development process and not included in the production build:

```
1  npm install eslint eslint-loader --save-dev
```

After the installation, the next step is to configure ESLint to specify the rules you want to enforce in your project. This is done by creating a .eslintrc file in the root of your project. An example configuration might look like this:

```
1   {
2     "parser": "babel-eslint",
3     "extends": "airbnb",
4     "env": {
5       "browser": true,
6       "node": true
7     },
8     "rules": {
9       "no-console": "off",
10      "indent": ["error", 2]
11    }
12  }
```

In this .eslintrc example, the parser is set to babel-eslint to allow ESLint to understand modern JavaScript syntax, it extends the Airbnb JavaScript style guide, and it specifies environments (browser and node) where the JavaScript code will run. Additionally, it customizes rules to allow console statements and enforce a two-space indentation.

Next, incorporate ESLint Loader into the Webpack configuration to automatically lint your JavaScript files during the build process. This is achieved by adding a module rule in the webpack.config.js file like so:

```
1   module.exports = {
2     // Other configuration settings
3     module: {
4       rules: [
5         {
6           test: /\.js$/,
7           exclude: /node_modules/,
8           use: [
9             'babel-loader',
10            'eslint-loader'
11          ]
12        }
13      ]
14    }
15  };
```

This configuration specifies that for all .js files, excluding those in the node_modules folder, Webpack should use both babel-loader and eslint-loader. It is crucial to ensure that eslint-loader is placed after other loaders that process JavaScript files, such as babel-loader, since ESLint should lint the final JavaScript output.

Running Webpack with this configuration will now also lint your
JavaScript code according to the rules specified in the `.eslintrc`
file. If ESLint finds any issues that violate the coding standards, it
will output the errors and warnings in the terminal. Here is an
example output when there's a linting error:

```
ERROR in ./src/index.js
Module Error (from ./node_modules/eslint-loader/index.js):

/src/index.js
  1:1  error  Unexpected console statement  no-console

  1 problem (1 error, 0 warnings)
```

Finally, to fully integrate ESLint into your development workflow,
consider adding scripts in your `package.json` to manually lint your
project or fix certain issues automatically. For instance:

```
1  "scripts": {
2    "lint": "eslint . --ext .js",
3    "lint:fix": "eslint . --ext .js --fix"
4  }
```

This setup allows you to run `npm run lint` to check your code for
linting errors and `npm run lint:fix` to automatically fix some of the
issues identified by ESLint.

Incorporating ESLint Loader into your Webpack setup helps to maintain high code quality by enforcing coding standards automatically
during the build process. By linting your JavaScript code, you can
catch common errors and potential issues early, leading to more stable and reliable code in production.

3.9   Custom Loaders: Creating Your Own

Loaders in Webpack serve as a fundamental mechanism for
transforming files and incorporating them into the dependency
graph. While a wide range of loaders are available to cater to most
common needs, there might be scenarios where the development of
a custom loader becomes necessary. This section will discuss the

process of creating a custom loader to address unique project requirements.

Creating a custom loader in Webpack involves understanding the Webpack loader API and the structure that loaders must follow. A loader is essentially a function that takes the source code of a file as its input and returns a new version of the code after applying some transformations.

Before writing a custom loader, it is important to be familiar with the signature of a loader function. The basic structure is as follows:

```
1   module.exports = function(source) {
2       // Transform the source
3       return source;
4   };
```

Within the loader function, the source argument represents the file content that the loader will process. This function must return the transformed source or a value that Webpack can further process.

To illustrate the creation of a custom loader, consider a scenario where all the string literals in JavaScript files need to be prefixed with a specific phrase. Here is how such a loader might be implemented:

```
1   module.exports = function(source) {
2       return source.replace(/"([^"]*)"/g, '"PREFIX:$1"');
3   };
```

This custom loader searches for all string literals in the source code and prefixes them with "PREFIX:". The regular expression / "([^"]*)" /g is utilized for finding string literals.

Once the custom loader is created, it needs to be integrated into the Webpack configuration. This is achieved by including the loader in the module.rules array in the Webpack configuration file. Assuming the custom loader is saved in a file named prefix-loader.js, the configuration would look like this:

```
1   module: {
2       rules: [
3           {
4               test: /\.js$/,
5               use: {
```

```
 6                loader: path.resolve('./path/to/prefix-loader.js')
 7            }
 8        }
 9    ]
10 }
```

This configuration specifies that for every .js file, the prefix-loader.js should be applied.

Developers might need to make their loaders asynchronous if the transformations are time-consuming or involve I/O operations. Webpack provides a way to handle such scenarios by using the this.async function inside the loader. Here is a brief example that demonstrates asynchronous handling:

```
1 module.exports = function(source) {
2     const callback = this.async();
3     someAsyncOperation(source, function(err, result) {
4         if(err) return callback(err);
5         callback(null, result);
6     });
7 };
```

In this scenario, this.async returns a callback function that should be called with the resulting source once the asynchronous operation is completed.

When developing custom loaders, it is crucial to ensure that they are stateless and do not keep a state between different invocations. This ensures compatibility with Webpack's caching mechanisms and contributes to more predictable build outcomes.

While the availability of numerous loaders makes Webpack a powerful tool, the ability to create custom loaders provides developers with the flexibility to handle any special requirements their projects may have. Following the guidelines outlined above, developers can effectively extend Webpack's functionality to meet the unique needs of their applications.

3.10   Chaining Loaders for Complex Processing

In this section, we will discuss the concept and practical application of chaining loaders in Webpack, an advanced technique that enables sequential processing of modules through multiple loaders. This process is instrumental for complex scenarios where a single file type requires multiple transformations or when files depend on a series of processing steps before they can be integrated into the Webpack bundle.

A critical aspect to understand about loader chaining in Webpack is that it operates in a right-to-left or bottom-to-top order. This means that the last loader in the array is applied first, and the output of this loader is fed as input to the next loader in the sequence.

Consider the following Webpack configuration snippet as an example:

```
1   module.exports = {
2     module: {
3       rules: [
4         {
5           test: /\.scss$/,
6           use: [
7             'style-loader',
8             'css-loader',
9             'sass-loader'
10          ]
11        }
12      ]
13    }
14  };
```

In this configuration, three loaders are chained to process SCSS files. The process starts with the sass-loader, which compiles SCSS to CSS. The output CSS is then passed to the css-loader, which resolves @import and url() paths and outputs JavaScript modules. Finally, the style-loader injects the CSS into the DOM by creating a <style> tag. The order of loaders is crucial here: reversing the order would cause the process to fail since each loader expects a specific input format.

Chaining loaders allows Webpack to handle more complex transformation and optimization tasks. However, it also requires careful setup and management. To optimize this process, consider the following practices:

- **Debugging**: Debugging issues in a chain of loaders can be challenging. Start by isolating the problem to a specific loader in the chain. This can be done by temporarily removing or replacing loaders to see how the output changes.

- **Order of Loaders**: Always be mindful of the order in which loaders are applied. This order directly influences the outcome of the processing chain.

- **Loader Options**: Many loaders offer a range of options for customization. Leverage these options to finely tune the behavior of each loader in the chain for optimal results.

- **Performance**: While chaining multiple loaders can solve complex processing requirements, it can also impact build performance. Evaluate the necessity of each loader in the chain and consider alternatives that may offer better performance.

To further illustrate the importance of correct loader sequencing, let's take a closer look at a hypothetical output of the aforementioned SCSS processing chain:

```
<style>
body {
  background-color: #00ff00;
}
</style>
```

This simple output demonstrates the end result of a successful loader chain: SCSS code is transformed into executable JavaScript that, when run in the browser, dynamically injects a `<style>` tag with the compiled CSS. Errors in the loader sequence would prevent this result, showcasing the delicate balance required in loader configuration.

In summary, chaining loaders is a powerful feature in Webpack that enables complex processing scenarios. Correct configuration, mindful management of loader order, and optimization for performance are key to leveraging this feature effectively.

3.11 Troubleshooting Common Loader Issues

Troubleshooting is an inevitable part of working with Webpack loaders. Despite thorough configuration, developers may encounter issues that impede progress. Recognizing and resolving common loader-related problems ensures a smoother development process. This section focuses on identifying and troubleshooting prevalent loader issues within a Webpack environment.

Module Not Found Error

A frequent issue encountered is the `Module not found` error. This typically occurs when Webpack is unable to locate a file or module specified in an import or require statement. The error message will usually point to the problematic file or dependency.

To resolve `Module not found` errors, verify the following:

- The path to the module is correct and accurately reflects the file structure.

- The file or package being imported exists and is not accidentally deleted or moved.

- For npm packages, ensure the package is properly installed by checking the `node_modules` directory or running `npm install` to fetch missing dependencies.

Incorrect Loader Configuration

Issues may also arise from misconfigurations within the
webpack.config.js file. An incorrectly set up loader can lead to
unexpected behavior, such as styles not being applied or images not
displaying.

When facing configuration issues, consider the following steps for
debugging:

- Double-check that the loader is installed locally within the
  project. Running npm list <loader_name> can confirm its
  presence.

- Examine the rules array within the module section of the
  webpack.config.js file. Ensure that the test patterns (regular
  expressions) correctly match the file types you intend to
  process with the loader.

- Validate the options provided to loaders for accuracy and compatibility. Some loaders may require specific version ranges of
  Webpack or other dependencies.

Conflicting Loaders

Loaders can sometimes interfere with each other, especially if multiple loaders are configured to process the same type of files. This can
result in compilation errors or unexpected output.

To avoid or resolve conflicts between loaders, follow these
guidelines:

- Explicitly specify the order of loaders. Webpack processes loaders in reverse order, from last to first in the use array. Consider
  which loader should apply its transformations first.

- Utilize the exclude and include options to narrowly target
  files for each loader, preventing overlap in processing.

- When using `oneOf` within the `rules` array, ensure that only one loader matches a given file. `oneOf` allows for conditional loader application, reducing the chance of conflicts.

Performance Issues

Performance issues can manifest when processing a large number of assets or when loaders are improperly configured. Slow build times and increased memory usage are common symptoms.

To enhance performance, consider the following adjustments:

- Use the `cache` option for loaders that support it. Caching allows previously processed files to be skipped, speeding up subsequent builds.

- Limit the scope of loaders with `include` or `exclude`, reducing unnecessary file processing.

- Evaluate the necessity of each loader and remove any that are redundant or unused.

By understanding and applying these troubleshooting techniques, developers can effectively resolve common issues encountered when working with Webpack loaders, leading to a more efficient and error-free development environment.

3.12 Loader Best Practices: Efficiency and Maintenance

Efficiency and maintenance are pivotal in managing loaders within the Webpack configuration. By adopting a series of best practices, developers can ensure their projects are both performant and easy to maintain. This section outlines actionable strategies to achieve these objectives.

- **Minimize the Use of Loaders**: It's important to apply loaders only when necessary. Over-utilizing loaders can lead to inflated build times and reduced project performance. Consider the exact requirements of your project and use loaders judiciously to transform the necessary files.

- **Loader Specificity**: Specify loaders as narrowly as possible. Instead of applying a loader globally, scope its application to the files or directories where it is needed. This can be done by defining test patterns and include/exclude options in the loader configuration.

```
1   module: {
2     rules: [
3       {
4         test: /\.css$/,
5         use: ['style-loader', 'css-loader'],
6         include: path.resolve(__dirname, 'src/styles'),
7       },
8     ],
9   }
```

- **Employing Caching**: Some loaders offer caching options to store the results of costly operations. For loaders like `babel-loader`, enabling caching can significantly reduce compilation times during development.

```
1   {
2     loader: 'babel-loader',
3     options: {
4       cacheDirectory: true
5     }
6   }
```

- **Order of Loaders**: The order in which loaders are applied is crucial. Webpack processes loaders right-to-left (or bottom-to-top). Understanding this sequencing is essential when chaining loaders, ensuring transformations occur in the correct order.

```
1   use: [
2     'style-loader',
3     'css-loader',
4     'sass-loader'
5   ]
```

- **Version Management**: Keep loaders up to date. Loader updates can bring optimizations, security patches, and new features beneficial to your project. Use tools such as npm or yarn to manage and update your dependencies regularly.

- **Use Loader Defaults Where Possible**: Many loaders come with sensible defaults. Before customizing, evaluate if the default configuration meets the project's needs, potentially reducing complexity.

- **Creating Custom Loaders**: For unique project requirements, creating a custom loader may be necessary. Adhere to Webpack's guidelines for writing loaders, focusing on stateless, deterministic functions that cache results whenever feasible.

```
1   module.exports = function(source) {
2     const result = customTransform(source);
3     this.cacheable && this.cacheable();
4     return result;
5   };
```

Lastly, frequent documentation review is recommended. The Webpack ecosystem evolves, and staying informed about the latest loader recommendations, deprecated features, and emerging best practices is beneficial.

In summary, by implementing these best practices, developers can ensure their Webpack configurations are both efficient and easy to maintain, providing a stable foundation for development and production builds.

Chapter 4

Integrating Plugins

Plugins augment the capabilities of Webpack beyond asset bundling, enabling a wide range of additional functionalities such as bundle optimization, environment variable injection, and automated file management. This chapter provides an in-depth examination of how to effectively integrate plugins into a Webpack configuration. Covering essential plugins like HtmlWebpackPlugin, MiniCssExtractPlugin, and CleanWebpackPlugin, it guides readers through the process of enhancing their build process. From installation and configuration to custom plugin development, this chapter equips readers with the knowledge to leverage plugins for more refined control over the compilation and optimization of their projects.

4.1 Exploring the Power of Plugins in Webpack

Plugins in Webpack serve as the backbone for extending the functionality of the Webpack ecosystem. By definition, a plugin is a JavaScript object that hooks into the Webpack compilation process, offering the ability to customize and manipulate the build according to specific needs. This flexibility makes plugins an indispensable part of modern web development workflows.

To integrate a plugin with Webpack, it is imperative to first understand the basic structure of a plugin. A Webpack plugin typically follows a specific pattern, characterized by:

- A JavaScript class that encapsulates the functionality of the plugin.

- A required `apply` method that Webpack calls during the compilation process.

- Access to the entire compilation lifecycle through the `compiler` object passed to the `apply` method, which allows the plugin to hook into various stages of the build process.

An elementary example of a custom plugin might look like this:

```
class HelloWorldPlugin {
  apply(compiler) {
    compiler.hooks.done.tap('Hello World Plugin', (
      stats /* stats is an object containing information about the completed
             compilation */
    ) => {
      console.log('Hello World!');
    });
  }
}
```

This plugin, though simplistic, demonstrates the crucial components of a Webpack plugin: the class structure and the `apply` method. When integrated within a Webpack configuration, it prints "Hello World!" to the console at the end of the compilation.

Integration of the plugin into the Webpack configuration involves adding it to the `plugins` array within the `webpack.config.js` file, as illustrated below:

```
const HelloWorldPlugin = require('./HelloWorldPlugin');

module.exports = {
  // Other Webpack configuration options
  plugins: [
```

```
6        new HelloWorldPlugin()
7      ]
8    };
```

Once integrated, running the Webpack build process invokes the plugin, executing its functionality at the specified compilation stage.

The power of plugins within Webpack lies in their capacity for customization. From performance optimizations, such as tree shaking and code splitting, to functional enhancements like dynamic HTML generation or environment variable injection, plugins can significantly elevate the development and build process. Some well-known plugins in the Webpack ecosystem include:

- HtmlWebpackPlugin for generating HTML files to serve your bundles

- MiniCssExtractPlugin for extracting CSS into separate files

- CleanWebpackPlugin for cleaning up the /dist folder before each build

- ImageMinimizerPlugin for optimizing image files

Understanding and harnessing the power of plugins is crucial for any developer looking to maximize the efficiency and performance of their Webpack builds. Through exploring the range of plugins available and learning to integrate them effectively into the compilation process, developers can significantly enhance the functionality and efficiency of their web applications.

4.2 Setting Up the HtmlWebpackPlugin for Dynamic HTML

The HtmlWebpackPlugin simplifies the creation of HTML files to serve your bundles. It particularly becomes indispensable when working with Webpack, as it dynamically injects script tags into your HTML file during the build process. This functionality ensures that every compilation produces an HTML file that references the latest bundles, thus automating an aspect of file management that is prone to human error.

To begin the integration of HtmlWebpackPlugin into a Webpack setup, one must first install the plugin. This is accomplished by running the following command in the terminal:

```
1  npm install --save-dev html-webpack-plugin
```

After installation, the plugin must then be activated and configured within the Webpack configuration file, traditionally named webpack.config.js. To do this, require the plugin at the top of your configuration file and include an instance of it in the plugins array as shown below:

```
1   const HtmlWebpackPlugin = require('html-webpack-plugin');
2
3   module.exports = {
4     plugins: [
5       new HtmlWebpackPlugin({
6         template: './src/index.html',
7         filename: 'index.html'
8       })
9     ]
10  };
```

In the configuration example above, two primary options are set for HtmlWebpackPlugin:

- template: This specifies the path to the HTML template file that serves as a basis for the output HTML. The path is relative to the location of the webpack.config.js file.

- filename: Defines the name of the file to be generated. This file will be placed in the output directory specified by the Webpack configuration, which is 'dist' by default unless changed.

With these settings, HtmlWebpackPlugin will generate an HTML file based on the specified template and automatically inject script tags that reference the output bundles generated by Webpack.

An essential feature of using HtmlWebpackPlugin is dynamic script injection. This ensures that each build's output, potentially with different hash values for filenames if content hashing is used, is correctly referenced in the HTML file. Consequently, manual updates to the HTML file to point to new script or asset versions are no longer necessary, significantly reducing the potential for errors and simplifying the development process.

The inclusion of additional options can further refine how HtmlWebpackPlugin operates. For instance, setting the `minify` option to `true` instructs the plugin to minify the resulting HTML file, a practice that can contribute to reduced file sizes and faster load times in a production environment.

```
1  new HtmlWebpackPlugin({
2    template: './src/index.html',
3    filename: 'index.html',
4    minify: true
5  })
```

In summary, the integration of HtmlWebpackPlugin into a Webpack configuration streamlines the production of HTML files and the management of script tag injections. This automation facilitates a smoother development workflow and ensures that the final HTML always references the correct version of bundle files. Furthermore, the plugin supports a range of options that offer control over the output, making it a powerful tool for optimizing the preparation of HTML files in a Webpack-based project.

4.3   Enhancing CSS Processing with MiniCs-sExtractPlugin

MiniCssExtractPlugin is a plugin for Webpack that extracts CSS into separate files. It generates a CSS file per JS file which contains CSS. This is beneficial for CSS and source maps' caching and parallel loading. The plugin is crucial for those targeting production build processes where performance is a key concern.

Let's start with the installation process. The MiniCssExtractPlugin is available through npm and can be installed using the command:

```
1  npm install --save-dev mini-css-extract-plugin
```

Once installed, the plugin must be included and configured in your Webpack configuration. Import the plugin at the top of the Webpack configuration file:

```
1   const MiniCssExtractPlugin = require('mini-css-extract-plugin');
```

Integration of MiniCssExtractPlugin into the Webpack configuration involves a few critical steps:

- Adding the plugin to the array of plugins in your Webpack configuration.

- Modifying the rules for CSS files to use MiniCssExtractPlugin's loader.

Here is a snippet showcasing how to add the plugin to your Webpack configuration:

```
1   plugins: [
2       new MiniCssExtractPlugin({
3           filename: '[name].[contenthash].css',
4       }),
5   ],
```

The `filename` option specifies the name of the output CSS file. `[name]` and `[contenthash]` tokens can be used within the name to include the name of the entry point and a hash of the content for cache busting, respectively.

Next, you will need to adjust Webpack's module rules to use the MiniCssExtractPlugin's loader for CSS files. This involves replacing style-loader with MiniCssExtractPlugin.loader in the rules for processing CSS files:

```
1   module: {
2       rules: [
3           {
4               test: /\.css$/,
5               use: [
6                   MiniCssExtractPlugin.loader,
7                   'css-loader'
8               ],
9           },
```

```
10    ],
11    },
```

Here, \.css$ is a regular expression that matches any files ending in .css. The use array specifies that MiniCssExtractPlugin's loader should be used first to process these files, followed by 'css-loader'.

This configuration extracts CSS from your bundle into separate files, enhancing load times and caching effectiveness. Furthermore, it facilitates the use of source maps for CSS, improving the developer experience by making debugging easier.

Deploying MiniCssExtractPlugin in your Webpack setup empowers you to optimize CSS delivery, which is vital for creating fast and responsive web applications. Carefully managing your CSS and leveraging Webpack's powerful ecosystem can significantly enhance the performance and maintainability of your projects.

4.4 Optimizing Assets with ImageMinimizerPlugin

Image assets play a critical role in web development, impacting both the visual appeal and the load time of a website. High-quality images often come with a significant overhead, leading to slow page loads and a suboptimal user experience. To address this challenge, the ImageMinimizerPlugin becomes an indispensable tool in the arsenal of modern web developers. This plugin integrates seamlessly into the Webpack build process, offering a comprehensive solution for image optimization that reduces file sizes without compromising image quality.

The first step in leveraging the ImageMinimizerPlugin is to install it along with its required dependencies. This can be achieved via npm or yarn. The following code snippet demonstrates the installation command:

```
1   npm install image-minimizer-webpack-plugin imagemin imagemin-mozjpeg imagemin-
        pngquant --save-dev
```

Upon successful installation, the next phase involves integrating the plugin into the Webpack configuration file. This integration is critical for instructing Webpack on when and how to apply image optimizations. The following example illustrates a basic integration within a Webpack configuration:

```
1   const ImageMinimizerPlugin = require('image-minimizer-webpack-plugin');
2
3   module.exports = {
4     // Your existing Webpack configuration
5     plugins: [
6       // Other plugins
7       new ImageMinimizerPlugin({
8         minimizerOptions: {
9           plugins: [
10            ['imagemin-mozjpeg', { quality: 75 }],
11            ['imagemin-pngquant', { quality: [0.6, 0.8] }]
12          ],
13        },
14      }),
15    ],
16  };
```

The plugin configuration options allow for extensive customization. In this case, `imagemin-mozjpeg` and `imagemin-pngquant` are specified as the chosen optimization algorithms, with quality settings tailored to balance between compression and image fidelity.

One critical aspect of the `ImageMinimizerPlugin` is its capability to operate in two distinct modes: `lossy` and `lossless`. Lossy compression reduces file sizes by slightly lowering image quality—a change often imperceptible to the naked eye. Conversely, lossless compression retains the original image quality by removing unnecessary metadata and optimizing encoding. The choice between these modes depends on the project requirements and the desired outcome in terms of image quality and file size.

To ensure the deployment of optimized images across all environments, it is essential to integrate the `ImageMinimizerPlugin` as part of the continuous integration (CI) pipeline. This practice helps in maintaining a consistent quality standard and speed optimization, reinforcing the importance of image optimization in modern web development.

```
Before Optimization:
```

```
- Image1.jpg: 300KB
- Image2.png: 450KB

After Optimization:
- Image1.jpg: 120KB
- Image2.png: 175KB
```

The code output example above showcases the effectiveness of the `ImageMinimizerPlugin`, illustrating substantial reductions in file sizes post-optimization. Such optimizations directly contribute to enhanced page loading speeds and improved overall user experience.

The integration and configuration of the `ImageMinimizerPlugin` within a Webpack build process enable developers to efficiently tackle the challenge of image file size without sacrificing quality. This plugin not only automates the optimization process but also provides a flexible framework for customization, making it an essential component for any project aiming to deliver high-quality web experiences.

4.5 Improving Caching with HashedModuleIdsPlugin

Improving the effectiveness of caching is crucial in web development, especially for applications with large amounts of static assets that do not change frequently. Webpack offers a solution for this through the `HashedModuleIdsPlugin`. This plugin ensures that file names are consistent between builds for files that have not changed, making it easier for web browsers to cache these files and improving load times for end-users.

By default, Webpack assigns incremental identifiers to modules when it builds the bundle. These identifiers can change between builds, even if the module itself has not changed. This behavior invalidates cache for unchanged assets, which is not ideal from a performance perspective. The `HashedModuleIdsPlugin` addresses this issue by generating a hash based on the module path. This hash remains the same as long as the file content does not change, thus enabling more effective caching by the browser.

To integrate the `HashedModuleIdsPlugin` into a Webpack configuration, follow these steps:

```
1   const webpack = require('webpack');
2
3   module.exports = {
4     // Other Webpack configuration properties
5     plugins: [
6       new webpack.HashedModuleIdsPlugin({
7         hashFunction: 'sha256',
8         hashDigest: 'hex',
9         hashDigestLength: 20
10      })
11    ]
12  };
```

In the code snippet above, the plugin is initialized with a set of options:

- `hashFunction`: Specifies the algorithm used for generating the hash. Popular options include `md5`, `sha256`, and `sha512`.

- `hashDigest`: Defines the encoding to use for the hash. Common encodings are `hex`, `base64`, and `latin1`.

- `hashDigestLength`: Determines the length of the hash. A longer hash reduces the possibility of hash collisions but results in longer filenames.

It is essential to understand the impact of each option on the caching strategy and to balance between the uniqueness of module identifiers and the conciseness of the generated filenames.

The effectiveness of caching can be evaluated using browser dev tools to inspect the network requests. If properly configured, files that have not changed between deployments should have their cache utilized, reducing the number of network requests and thereby enhancing the application's load time.

The `HashedModuleIdsPlugin` plays a pivotal role in optimizing the caching strategy of a Webpack-compiled application. By ensuring that unchanged modules retain consistent identifiers across builds, this plugin contributes significantly to improving the performance and user experience of web applications.

4.6 Automating Cleaning of the /dist Folder with CleanWebpackPlugin

When working with Webpack, the output directory (commonly the /dist folder) serves as the destination for all compiled and bundled assets. Over time, as the project evolves, this folder becomes cluttered with outdated versions of assets, potentially leading to confusion during deployment or development. To address this issue, CleanWebpackPlugin comes into play. It is specifically designed to automate the cleaning of the /dist folder before each build, ensuring that only the latest assets are deployed.

To integrate CleanWebpackPlugin into a Webpack configuration, you must first install the plugin. Assuming you have Webpack already configured in your project, you can add CleanWebpackPlugin by running the following command in your project's root directory:

```
1  npm install clean-webpack-plugin --save-dev
```

After the installation is complete, import CleanWebpackPlugin into your Webpack configuration file. The plugin is imported from the 'clean-webpack-plugin' package. Here is a simple example of how to import and configure CleanWebpackPlugin in the Webpack configuration file:

```
1  const { CleanWebpackPlugin } = require('clean-webpack-plugin');
2
3  module.exports = {
4    // Other configuration options...
5    plugins: [
6      new CleanWebpackPlugin(),
7      // Other plugins...
8    ],
9  };
```

105

Upon integration, CleanWebpackPlugin will automatically remove all files inside the /dist folder every time the build process is initiated, leaving only the latest build outputs. This behavior helps in maintaining a clean workspace and prevents potential conflicts or confusions arising from stale files.

One of the key features of CleanWebpackPlugin is its configurability. While the default settings are adequate for most projects, CleanWebpackPlugin allows for customization to fit specific requirements. For instance, to clean specific directories or to maintain certain files despite the cleaning process, configuration options can be provided to the plugin, as shown below:

```
1  new CleanWebpackPlugin({
2    // Clean specific paths.
3    cleanOnceBeforeBuildPatterns: ['**/*', '!static-files*', '!.
        gitignore'],
4  }),
```

In this configuration example, all files in the /dist folder will be removed except for those in the 'static-files' directory and the '.gitignore' file. This level of customizability allows developers significant control over the cleaning process, ensuring that only undesired files are removed.

It's important to note that use of CleanWebpackPlugin enhances the development process by maintaining a clean build directory, but it should be configured with caution, especially when setting custom patterns, to avoid unintentional deletion of essential files.

CleanWebpackPlugin serves as a critical tool in automating the maintenance of the /dist folder, streamlining the build process, and ensuring the deployment of fresh assets. Its inclusion in the Webpack configuration simplifies the developer's workflow and contributes to the efficiency and reliability of the project build cycle.

4.7 Code Analysis with BundleAnalyzerPlugin

The BundleAnalyzerPlugin stands as a significant instrument for optimizing the webpack build process through comprehensive analysis of the bundled assets. It furnishes developers with a visual depiction of the contents of their bundles, facilitating the identification of potential optimizations by highlighting the sizes of the included modules and their contributions to the overall bundle size. This feature is instrumental in pinpointing redundant or unnecessary code, allowing for a more streamlined and efficient build.

To incorporate the BundleAnalyzerPlugin into a webpack project, it is necessary to first install it. This is achieved via the npm package manager. The command for installation is as follows:

```
npm install --save-dev webpack-bundle-analyzer
```

Upon successful installation, the next step involves integrating the plugin into the webpack configuration file. This is accomplished by importing the plugin and incorporating it into the plugins array within the webpack configuration object. An illustrative example of this process is provided below:

```
const { BundleAnalyzerPlugin } = require('webpack-bundle-analyzer');

module.exports = {
    // Other webpack configuration settings
    plugins: [
        new BundleAnalyzerPlugin({
            analyzerMode: 'server',
            analyzerHost: '127.0.0.1',
            analyzerPort: 8888,
            openAnalyzer: true,
        }),
        // Other plugins
    ],
};
```

In the configuration for BundleAnalyzerPlugin, several options are available to customize its behavior. The analyzerMode option can be set to 'server', 'static', or 'disabled'. Selecting 'server' launches a local web server that displays the bundle report in a browser. The analyzerHost and analyzerPort options specify the host and port for the web server, respectively, while openAnalyzer controls whether the report is automatically opened in the browser.

Once the plugin is properly configured, executing the webpack build process generates a detailed report of the bundle contents. The output visualizes each module's size, allowing developers to identify and address issues related to bundle size effectively. The utility of the BundleAnalyzerPlugin extends beyond mere size metrics; it also aids in the detection of duplicate packages and potential bottlenecks in the build process.

For further customization and advanced analysis, developers can explore additional configuration options provided by the BundleAnalyzerPlugin. These include the ability to generate static reports in HTML format, filter modules from the visualization, and adjust the graphical representation of the bundles. The versatility and granular control offered by the BundleAnalyzerPlugin make it an indispensable tool for optimizing webpack builds, enhancing application performance, and ensuring the efficient delivery of resources to users.

4.8   Hot Module Replacement with HMR Plugin

Hot Module Replacement (HMR) is a mechanism offered by Webpack to inject updated modules into the current application session. This feature significantly enhances the development experience by allowing changes to be seen without a full browser refresh, which can disrupt application state and introduce latency. This section will delve into the integration of the HMR plugin within a Webpack configuration.

To activate HMR in your project, it is necessary to modify both your Webpack configuration and development server settings. The following steps outline the process:

- Install the necessary packages by running the command npm install --save-dev webpack-dev-server.

- Incorporate the webpack-dev-server into your Webpack configuration file.

- Enable the hot property within the devServer configuration.

Here is an exemplified configuration adjustment demonstrating how to activate HMR:

```
// webpack.config.js
const webpack = require('webpack');

module.exports = {
    entry: './src/index.js',
    output: {
        path: __dirname + '/dist',
        filename: 'bundle.js'
    },
    devServer: {
        contentBase: './dist',
        hot: true
    },
    plugins: [
        new webpack.HotModuleReplacementPlugin()
    ]
};
```

The configuration above performs several key tasks:

- It specifies an entry point './src/index.js' from where the bundling process begins.

- The output section defines the destination (path) for the generated bundle and its filename (filename).

- Within the devServer section, contentBase is set to the './dist' directory, indicating where to serve the files from. The hot property activates the Hot Module Replacement feature.

- Finally, the new webpack.HotModuleReplacementPlugin() is added to the plugins array to enable HMR in your Webpack build.

Upon implementation, when running the command npm start (assuming it's configured to launch your development server), Webpack compiles your assets and serves them. Once a file is modified, the HMR Plugin updates the application with new modules.   This may be observed without a full page reload, enhancing efficiency in development.

```
[HMR] Waiting for update signal from WDS...
[WDS] Hot Module Replacement enabled.
```

The console output above signals the successful activation of HMR in your project, showcasing messages from both the Webpack Hot Module Replacement plugin (HMR) and Webpack Development Server (WDS).

It's essential to note that not all modules can be hot-reloaded out of the box. For instance, updating React component state without losing state requires integration with React Hot Loader or leveraging React Fast Refresh. Similar considerations apply for other frameworks and libraries as well, indicating the necessity for additional setup or plugins to fully utilize HMR capabilities according to specific development needs.

Integrating Hot Module Replacement into your Webpack setup offers a seamless experience for viewing code changes in real-time without the inconvenience of page reloads. By following the outlined steps and considering the compatibility of HMR with your project's stack, you can significantly streamline your development process.

4.9   Environment Plugin for Managing Environment Variables

Managing environment variables is a critical aspect of modern web development, especially when differentiating between development and production environments. The EnvironmentPlugin, offered by Webpack, is a built-in solution that simplifies the process of accessing environment variables in your application's code.

To utilize the EnvironmentPlugin, it must first be included in your Webpack configuration file. This is achieved by requiring the plugin from Webpack's module within the configuration file. The following code snippet demonstrates the inclusion of the EnvironmentPlugin:

```
const webpack = require('webpack');

module.exports = {
  // Other configuration settings...
  plugins: [
    new webpack.EnvironmentPlugin(['NODE_ENV', 'DEBUG'])
  ]
};
```

In the example above, the `EnvironmentPlugin` is instantiated with an array containing the names of environment variables that you intend to pass to your application from the process's environment. In this case, NODE_ENV and DEBUG are the specified environment variables. If any of these variables are not set in the process environment, Webpack will throw an error unless a default value is provided.

To provide default values for the environment variables, you can pass an object instead of an array to the `EnvironmentPlugin`, as shown in the following snippet:

```
new webpack.EnvironmentPlugin({
  NODE_ENV: 'development', // use 'development' unless process.env.NODE_ENV is
      defined
  DEBUG: false
});
```

By specifying default values, you ensure that your application has access to these environment variables even if they are not explicitly set in your development or CI/CD environment.

Accessing these environment variables in your application code is straightforward. Since the `EnvironmentPlugin` makes them available on the `process.env` object, you can simply refer to them as you would to any property on an object:

```
console.log('Environment:', process.env.NODE_ENV);
console.log('Debug mode:', process.env.DEBUG);
```

The output of these console log statements will reflect the values of the environment variables as they are set in the environment running your Webpack build, or their default values as defined in your Webpack configuration.

The EnvironmentPlugin is a powerful tool for managing environment variables, promoting clarity and maintainability in your application's configuration. It reduces boilerplate code associated with manually defining each environment variable and gracefully handles missing variables with default values or clear error messages.

Incorporating the EnvironmentPlugin into your Webpack setup ensures that your application is aware of its operational context, facilitating development practices that differentiate between various environments like development, staging, and production. This is crucial for making application behavior dynamic and adaptable to the conditions under which it is running, thereby enhancing the overall robustness and flexibility of your web application.

4.10   Compression and Optimization with CompressionWebpackPlugin

Optimizing the size of the assets is crucial for improving the load time of web applications. The CompressionWebpackPlugin is a powerful tool that facilitates this optimization by compressing the output assets of the Webpack build. This section will discuss the installation, configuration, and benefits of integrating CompressionWebpackPlugin into your Webpack setup.

First, to make CompressionWebpackPlugin available in your project, you need to install it through npm or yarn. The command for installation via npm is provided below:

```
1   npm install compression-webpack-plugin --save-dev
```

Once installed, integrating CompressionWebpackPlugin into your Webpack configuration requires importing the plugin and adding it to the plugins array in your webpack.config.js file. A basic setup

112

is shown in the following code snippet:

```
1  const CompressionPlugin = require('compression-webpack-plugin');
2
3  module.exports = {
4    // Other configuration options...
5    plugins: [
6      new CompressionPlugin({
7        algorithm: 'gzip',
8        test: /\.js(\?.*)?$/i,
9        threshold: 10240,
10       minRatio: 0.8
11     })
12   ]
13 };
```

In this configuration, several options are specified:

- algorithm: Defines the compression algorithm to be used. The default value is 'gzip'.

- test: A RegExp that identifies the files to be compressed. In this case, it targets JavaScript files.

- threshold: Only assets bigger than this size (in bytes) will be processed. The default value is 0 bytes.

- minRatio: Only assets that compress better than this ratio will be affected. The default value is 0.8.

After configuring CompressionWebpackPlugin, running the Webpack build will generate compressed versions of your assets alongside the original files. For instance, if you have a main.js file, the plugin would produce an additional file named main.js.gz (assuming the gzip algorithm is used).

To verify the compression, the output before and after applying the plugin can be compared. An example output without compression is:

```
Asset     Size
main.js   1.2 MiB
```

And after enabling CompressionWebpackPlugin, the output might look like:

```
Asset          Size
main.js        1.2 MiB
main.js.gz     300 KiB
```

This indicates a significant reduction in file size, which directly contributes to faster load times when serving compressed assets to the user's browser.

In summary, `CompressionWebpackPlugin` is an essential tool for optimizing the size of your Webpack build's output. By compressing your assets, you can substantially improve your application's performance, providing a better user experience. The flexibility of this plugin allows it to be adjusted to fit the specific needs of any project, making it a vital part of any Webpack configuration focused on optimization and performance.

4.11   Extending Webpack with Custom Plugins

Extending the functionality of Webpack can be achieved through the development of custom plugins, providing unparalleled flexibility in customizing the build process. This involves understanding the Webpack plugin architecture and API, enabling the creation of bespoke solutions for project-specific requirements.

Webpack plugins operate on the principle of tapping into the various hooks provided by the Webpack compiler and compilation objects. These hooks can be manipulated to introduce new processes or modify existing ones during different phases of the compilation lifecycle.

To begin developing a custom plugin, one must first create a JavaScript class that defines the `apply` method. This method is automatically called by Webpack, and it receives an instance of the Webpack compiler as its argument. The compiler object provides access to the entire Webpack environment, and its hooks property can be used to tap into various events.

Consider the example of creating a simple plugin to log a message at the beginning of the compilation:

```
1  class SimpleLoggerPlugin {
2      apply(compiler) {
3          compiler.hooks.beforeRun.tap('SimpleLoggerPlugin', compilation => {
4              console.log('The compilation is starting!');
5          });
6      }
7  }
```

In this example, the SimpleLoggerPlugin class defines an apply method that taps into the beforeRun hook of the compiler. The hook is tapped with the name of the plugin and a function that executes the desired action, in this case, logging a message to the console.

To integrate this plugin into a Webpack configuration, it needs to be instantiated within the plugins array of the Webpack configuration object:

```
1  const SimpleLoggerPlugin = require('./SimpleLoggerPlugin');
2
3  module.exports = {
4      // Other configuration properties
5      plugins: [
6          new SimpleLoggerPlugin()
7      ]
8  };
```

Custom plugins can also interact with Webpack's data system and even modify the output assets. Here's an example that appends a custom banner comment to the top of every generated file:

```
1   class BannerPlugin {
2       apply(compiler) {
3           compiler.hooks.emit.tapAsync('BannerPlugin', (compilation, callback) => {
4               const banner = '// This is a custom banner\n';
5               Object.keys(compilation.assets).forEach(assetName => {
6                   const asset = compilation.assets[assetName];
7                   const source = asset.source();
8                   const banneredSource = banner + source;
9                   compilation.assets[assetName] = {
10                      source: () => banneredSource,
11                      size: () => banneredSource.length,
12                  };
13              });
14              callback();
15          });
16      }
17  }
```

This `BannerPlugin` taps into the `emit` hook, which is triggered after the compilation has created the output assets but before they are emitted to the output directory. It prepends a specified banner text to the source of every asset.

In these ways, custom plugins empower developers to tailor the Webpack build process to their specific requirements, extending its capabilities far beyond predefined configurations and presets.

4.12   Plugin Best Practices: Performance and Integration

Integrating plugins into a Webpack configuration necessitates a balance between enhancing functionality and maintaining optimal build performance. Adhering to best practices when working with Webpack plugins can significantly influence the efficiency of the build process and the overall project architecture. This section delineates strategies for achieving optimal performance and seamless integration of plugins within a Webpack environment.

Selective Plugin Usage

First and foremost, it is crucial to adopt a minimalist approach to plugin inclusion. Only integrate plugins that offer indispensable functionality or a substantial improvement in development experience. This can be achieved by:

- Assessing the necessity of each plugin by critically evaluating if the desired functionality can't be achieved through Webpack's core features or simpler configurations.

- Reviewing and benchmarking alternatives to select the most performance-efficient plugin.

Analyzing Build Performance

Regularly analyze the impact of plugins on build times to identify performance bottlenecks. Webpack's `--profile` and `--json` commands can be utilized to generate detailed build statistics that can be further analyzed using tools like `webpack-bundle-analyzer`. For instance:

```
1  webpack --profile --json > stats.json
```

This generates a `stats.json` file, which can be visualized using:

```
1  webpack-bundle-analyzer stats.json
```

Lazy Loading

For web applications, particularly those with a vast number of modules, lazy loading can significantly enhance runtime performance. This refers to the practice of loading modules on demand rather than at the initial load. While Webpack facilitates this through dynamic imports (`import()`), certain plugins can further optimize this process. For example, `react-loadable` and `@loadable/component` for React applications.

Environment-Specific Configuration

Different environments (e.g., development, testing, production) often require diverging plugin configurations. For instance, minification and optimization plugins are typically more beneficial in a production environment. To manage this, employ Webpack's environment-based configuration capabilities:

```
1  module.exports = (env) => {
2    return {
3      plugins: [
4        ...(env.production ? [new CleanWebpackPlugin()] : []),
5        ...(env.development ? [new webpack.HotModuleReplacementPlugin()] : []),
6        // Add other environment-specific plugins here
7      ],
8    };
9  };
```

117

This approach helps in tailoring the build process to the specific needs of each environment without cluttering the configuration file with conditional logic.

Up-To-Date Plugin Versions

Keeping plugins updated is pivotal for both security and performance. Developers frequently enhance plugins with optimizations and compatibility improvements. However, it's also important to validate the stability and compatibility of the updated versions before incorporating them into the project.

Custom Plugin Development

In scenarios where existing plugins do not satisfy project-specific needs, developing a custom Webpack plugin is a viable option. Adhere to Webpack's plugin interface guidelines and ensure that custom plugins are:

- Optimized for performance, avoiding unnecessary computational complexity.

- Thoroughly tested across different Webpack configurations and versions.

- Documented, specifying installation, configuration settings, and usage examples.

Integrating and managing plugins efficiently is a nuanced aspect of working with Webpack. By following the aforementioned best practices, developers can leverage the robust plugin ecosystem of Webpack to substantially enhance their build process and application performance without succumbing to potential pitfalls such as inflated build times or unmanageable configuration complexity.

Chapter 5

Optimizing Your Build: Performance Techniques

Optimizing the performance of a Webpack build is crucial for creating fast and efficient web applications. This chapter focuses on advanced techniques and strategies to enhance the speed and size of your bundles. It covers a variety of optimization approaches, including code splitting, tree shaking, lazy loading, asset compression, and caching strategies. Each technique is explored in detail, providing practical insights on how to apply these optimizations to reduce load times and improve the overall user experience. By implementing these performance techniques, developers can significantly lower the resource footprint of their applications, ensuring they perform seamlessly across a wide range of devices and network conditions.

5.1 The Importance of Build Optimization

Optimizing the build process in a Webpack environment is a critical step for developers aiming to enhance the performance and efficiency of their web applications. Build optimization refers to the suite of techniques used to minimize the size of the generated bundles and to improve the loading and execution time of web applications. In a landscape where user experience can significantly impact the success of a web application, optimization plays a pivotal role in ensuring that applications are not only functional but also fast and responsive.

- **Improved Loading Times:** Optimizing your build can significantly reduce the load time of your web application. By implementing strategies such as code splitting and lazy loading, critical resources are prioritized, and non-essential resources are loaded asynchronously or on demand. This ensures that the initial load time, which is crucial for user retention, is as fast as possible.

- **Enhanced User Experience:** A faster web application contributes to a better user experience. Users are known to prefer websites and applications that load quickly and respond promptly to interactions. Optimization reduces the time users spend waiting for content to appear, thus improving overall satisfaction and engagement.

- **Reduced Bandwidth Consumption:** By minimizing bundle sizes through techniques such as tree shaking and asset compression, the amount of data that needs to be transferred over the network decreases. This is particularly important for users with limited or metered internet connections, as it not only improves loading times but also reduces data consumption.

- **Improved Performance Across Devices:** Optimized applications are more likely to run smoothly across a wide range of devices, including those with limited processing power or memory. This democratizes access to the application, ensuring that it performs well regardless of the user's hardware.

- **Better Search Engine Rankings:** Search engines like Google consider page speed as a ranking factor. Optimized web applications tend to rank higher in search results, leading to increased visibility and potentially more users.

Implementing build optimization techniques can initially seem daunting due to the complexity of the tools and strategies involved. However, the return on investment is substantial. By dedicating time to understanding and applying these optimizations, developers can significantly improve the performance and user experience of their web applications. In the following sections, we will explore several optimization strategies, each contributing to the overall goal of creating efficient, fast-loading web applications.

5.2 Analyzing Bundle Size with Webpack Bundle Analyzer

One of the initial steps toward optimizing your build involves understanding its current state. This is where the Webpack Bundle Analyzer comes into play. It's a handy tool that visualizes the size of webpack output files with an interactive zoomable treemap. This visualization aids in identifying the largest contributors to the bundle size, making it easier to pinpoint areas for improvement.

To use the Webpack Bundle Analyzer, it must first be integrated into your project. This can be achieved by installing the package via npm or yarn:

```
1  npm install --save-dev webpack-bundle-analyzer
2  # or
3  yarn add --dev webpack-bundle-analyzer
```

After installation, you can modify your webpack configuration file to include the Bundle Analyzer plugin. Here's how you can do this:

```
1  const BundleAnalyzerPlugin = require('webpack-bundle-analyzer').
       BundleAnalyzerPlugin;
2
3  module.exports = {
4      plugins: [
5          new BundleAnalyzerPlugin()
6      ]
7  };
```

Once the plugin is integrated, running your build process again will automatically open a new browser window displaying the treemap visualization of your project's bundles. In this visualization, each rectangle represents a different asset in your bundles, with sizes proportional to the asset's size.

The Bundle Analyzer provides several key pieces of information:

- The total size of the webpack output, helping you assess the weight of your application.

- A visual representation of each module within the bundle, making it straightforward to identify large dependencies.

- The ability to filter modules by size, allowing you to prioritize the most significant opportunities for optimization.

Analyzing the treemap can reveal surprising facts about your bundle. You may discover that a particular third-party library is significantly larger than expected, or that certain code paths are including unnecessary files. For instance, you might see output similar to the following for a particularly large module:

```
./node_modules/lodash/lodash.js 528 KB
```

Such insights are invaluable for making targeted optimizations. By identifying the largest modules, you can consider alternatives or look into code splitting to ensure they're only loaded when necessary.

Moreover, the Webpack Bundle Analyzer can be run in "static" mode, generating an HTML file you can inspect without starting a server. This is particularly useful for sharing insights with team members or embedding the report into continuous integration (CI) workflows. To generate a static report, you can modify the plugin's options as follows:

```
1  new BundleAnalyzerPlugin({
2      analyzerMode: 'static'
3  })
```

By harnessing the power of the Webpack Bundle Analyzer, developers gain a clearer understanding of their application's bundle size. This visibility is pivotal for making informed decisions that ultimately lead to significantly improved application performance. Through targeted optimizations guided by the analyzer's insights, developers can ensure their applications are lean, fast, and efficient.

5.3   Code Splitting: Concepts and Strategies

Code splitting is a key technique in optimizing web applications by dividing the codebase into smaller chunks or 'bundles'. Instead of serving a single large JavaScript file, code splitting allows developers to create multiple bundles that can be dynamically loaded at runtime. This approach significantly reduces the initial load time, as the browser can fetch only the necessary code for the current view or functionality, delaying the loading of other parts of the application until they are required.

To understand code splitting, it is essential to grasp the concept of "entry points" in the context of a Webpack configuration. An entry point defines the file or files that Webpack uses to start building the bundle. By default, Webpack creates a single bundle from a single entry point. However, specifying multiple entry points instructs Webpack to create a separate bundle for each entry point. This is the simplest form of code splitting.

Let's dive deeper into practical code splitting techniques:

- **Dynamic Imports:** JavaScript supports dynamic imports using the `import()` syntax. This feature allows chunks to be loaded on demand. For instance, if a particular piece of functionality is only needed under certain conditions or at a specific time, it can be loaded dynamically using `import()`.

```
1  // Example of dynamic import
2  button.onclick = () => {
3    import('./module.js')
4      .then(module => {
5        module.loadFunction();
6      })
7      .catch(err => {
```

```
8       console.error('Module loading failed:', err);
9     });
10  };
```

- **Vendor Chunk:** It is common practice to separate third-party libraries (the 'vendor' code) from the application code. Since vendor code changes less frequently, splitting it allows the browser to cache these libraries separately, reducing the amount of code that needs to be downloaded, parsed, and executed on subsequent visits.

```
1  // Webpack configuration for vendor splitting
2  module.exports = {
3    entry: {
4      main: './src/index.js',
5      vendor: ['lodash', 'moment'],
6    },
7    // Additional configuration...
8  };
```

- **React Lazy and Suspense:** For React applications, the React team introduced React.lazy and Suspense to facilitate code splitting at the component level. React.lazy allows dynamic imports of components, while Suspense provides a fallback UI during the loading process.

```
1  import React, { Suspense, lazy } from 'react';
2  const LazyComponent = lazy(() => import('./LazyComponent'));
3
4  function MyComponent() {
5    return (
6      <Suspense fallback={<div>Loading...</div>}>
7        <LazyComponent />
8      </Suspense>
9    );
10 }
```

Furthermore, when implementing code splitting, it is important to analyze the impact on performance. Tools like the Webpack Bundle Analyzer can provide visual feedback on the sizes of chunks, helping developers identify opportunities for optimization.

```
Webpack Bundle Analyzer output:
--------------------------------
- main.bundle.js  150KB
```

```
- vendor.bundle.js  300KB
- module.chunk.js  50KB
```

Code splitting is a powerful technique for improving the load time and runtime performance of web applications. By understanding and applying these strategies thoughtfully, developers can deliver a more responsive and efficient user experience.

5.4 Lazy Loading Components for Faster Initial Loads

Lazy loading is a design pattern aimed at reducing the size of the initially loaded web page by splitting the application bundle into smaller chunks and then loading pieces on demand rather than loading the entire application upfront. This technique can significantly decrease initial load times, improve user experience by making the application feel snappier, and ultimately contribute to the optimization of web resources.

To implement lazy loading in a Webpack-powered project, it is essential to understand the concept of dynamic imports. Dynamic imports allow you to define a point within your application where a certain module or component will only be loaded when it is needed.

Implementing Dynamic Imports

Dynamic imports in JavaScript can be utilized with the 'import()' syntax, which works similarly to the traditional 'import' statement but is called as a function and returns a promise. This promise resolves with the module when the module is successfully loaded.

Here is a basic example of how to use dynamic imports for lazy loading:

```
1  // Assume we have a component named `ExpensiveComponent.js` that we want to load
       lazily.
2  const loadExpensiveComponent = () => import('./ExpensiveComponent');
```

In the example above, 'loadExpensiveComponent' is a function that, when called, dynamically imports 'ExpensiveComponent.js'. Since 'import()' returns a promise, you can use '.then' to handle the module once it is loaded.

Integration with Webpack

Webpack integrates seamlessly with dynamic imports, automatically splitting your bundle into chunks. When Webpack encounters a dynamic import statement in your code, it creates a separate chunk file for the imported module. This process is known as code splitting.

```
1   // In your Webpack configuration, ensure chunk splitting is enabled.
2   optimization: {
3     splitChunks: {
4       chunks: 'all',
5     },
6   }
```

This configuration tells Webpack to split chunks out of the bundle. The 'chunks: 'all'' option specifies that both, for dynamically imported modules and for the initial bundle, chunks should be created.

Utilizing React.lazy for Component Lazy Loading

For projects using React, a convenient way to implement lazy loading is by using the 'React.lazy' function. It enables you to render a dynamic import as a regular component.

```
 1   import React, { Suspense } from 'react';
 2
 3   const LazyLoadedComponent = React.lazy(() => import('./ExpensiveComponent'));
 4
 5   function App() {
 6     return (
 7       <Suspense fallback={<div>Loading...</div>}>
 8         <LazyLoadedComponent />
 9       </Suspense>
10     );
11   }
```

In the snippet above, 'React.lazy' is used to dynamically import 'ExpensiveComponent', and 'Suspense' is used to wrap the lazy-loaded component, providing a fallback content (in this case, a loading message) while the component is being loaded.

Benefits of Lazy Loading

Implementing lazy loading can significantly impact the performance of a web application by reducing the initial load time. This is particularly beneficial for applications with a large number of components or those that include heavy libraries and frameworks not immediately needed upon the first visit. The reduced initial payload means faster rendering times and an improved user experience, especially for users on slow internet connections or devices with limited processing power.

Lazy loading is a powerful technique for optimizing web applications by reducing initial load times and conserving bandwidth. By strategically implementing lazy loading using dynamic imports and leveraging Webpack's code splitting capabilities, developers can create applications that are both high-performing and resource-efficient.

5.5 Tree Shaking to Remove Unused Code

Tree shaking is a term originally coined in the context of JavaScript bundling. It refers to the process of removing unused code from a bundle during the build process. This section will delve into the mechanism of tree shaking, its prerequisites for effective implementation, and ways to leverage it using Webpack to achieve a smaller bundle size and, consequently, improved application performance.

To understand tree shaking, it is critical to first encapsulate its principle in the context of module import and export. JavaScript modules can export multiple functions or variables, but only a subset of these exports might be used by other modules. Without tree shaking, all exports from a module would be included in the final bundle, regardless of whether they are used or not. This results in unnecessary bytes added to the bundle size, decreasing web performance. Tree shaking eliminates this overhead by including only used exports.

Enabling Tree Shaking in Webpack

To enable tree shaking in Webpack, certain conditions must be met:

- The application must use ES2015 module syntax (i.e., import and export).

- The Webpack configuration must specify the mode as 'production'. This enables built-in optimization features, including minification and tree shaking.

- The Babel configuration, if used, must be set up not to transform module syntax. The Babel preset option {"modules": false} prevents transformation of ES modules, thus preserving the import and export statements required for tree shaking.

Configuring Webpack for Tree Shaking

Below is an example Webpack configuration that ensures tree shaking is applied:

```
1   const path = require('path');
2
3   module.exports = {
4       entry: './src/index.js',
5       mode: 'production',
6       output: {
7           path: path.resolve(__dirname, 'dist'),
8           filename: 'bundle.js',
9       },
10      module: {
11          rules: [
12              {
13                  test: /\.js$/,
14                  exclude: /node_modules/,
15                  use: {
16                      loader: 'babel-loader',
17                      options: {
```

```
18          presets: [['@babel/preset-env', { modules: false }]]
19        }
20      }
21    },
22  ],
23  },
24 };
```

This configuration specifies 'production' mode optimizing the output bundle, including tree shaking. The Babel loader is configured to preserve ES2015 modules.

Verifying Tree Shaking

After configuring and building the project with Webpack, it's essential to verify that tree shaking is effectively removing unused code. This can be done by inspecting the final bundle. Webpack's terser plugin, used for minification in production mode, also aids by eliminating dead code. However, determining precisely which code was shaken off is more nuanced and may require analyzing the source and the resulting bundle.

Considerations for Effective Tree Shaking

While tree shaking is a powerful tool for reducing bundle size, its effectiveness hinges on a few considerations:

- Side effects in modules can hinder tree shaking. Webpack assumes every module could have side effects unless explicitly stated otherwise in the package's package.json file, using the "sideEffects": false property.

- Dynamically imported modules using import() syntax facilitate better tree shaking by splitting the codebase into chunks only loaded when needed.

- Reducing or eliminating unused code at the source, by ensuring that imports are as specific as possible and avoiding blanket imports, can further enhance tree shaking's benefits.

Implementing tree shaking requires careful setup and attention to detail in both code and configuration. However, the payoff in reduced bundle sizes and improved performance is significant, making it an essential optimization technique in modern web development.

5.6   Caching Strategies: Leveraging Browser Caching

Caching plays a pivotal role in enhancing web application performance by storing copies of files locally in a user's browser. This section will discuss leveraging browser caching to reduce load times and network traffic, improving the overall user experience.

The core idea behind browser caching is to store frequently accessed resources, such as JavaScript files, CSS stylesheets, and images, on the user's local machine after the first visit. When the user returns to the website, the browser can load these resources from the cache rather than downloading them again from the server. This mechanism significantly reduces the resources' load time, as local access is invariably faster than network requests.

To implement caching effectively, web developers need to understand and manipulate HTTP headers. Two primary HTTP headers influence browser caching: `Cache-Control` and `Expires`.

1. The `Cache-Control` Header

The `Cache-Control` header provides mechanisms to control caching directly. It offers several directives that can be used to fine-tune how and how long the resources are cached. Commonly used directives include:

- `max-age=[seconds]`: Specifies the maximum amount of time a resource is considered fresh.

- `no-cache`: Forces the browser to validate the resource with the server before using it.

- `no-store`: Instructs the browser not to cache the resource.

- `public`: Indicates that the response is cacheable by any cache.

- `private`: Specifies that the response is intended for a single user and should not be cached by shared caches.

An effective utilization of the `Cache-Control` header can be illustrated through an example:

```
Cache-Control: public, max-age=31536000
```

This directive indicates that a resource can be cached by any cache and has a maximum age of one year (31536000 seconds), making it an ideal setting for static resources like images or CSS files.

2. The `Expires` Header

The `Expires` header is used to define an explicit expiration time for a resource, after which it is considered stale. While `Cache-Control` is generally preferred due to its granularity and modern approach, the `Expires` header can be useful for HTTP/1.0 compatibility. An example of its usage is:

```
Expires: Wed, 21 Oct 2025 07:28:00 GMT
```

In this example, the resource is set to expire on 21st October 2025, indicating to the browser that it can safely cache the resource until this date.

Strategies for Leveraging Browser Caching

Implementing browser caching requires a strategic approach to ensure that users benefit from faster load times without serving outdated content. Some strategies include:

- Using versioning or fingerprinting on filenames of cacheable resources. This approach involves appending a version number or hash to the filename, prompting the browser to re-fetch the resource when it changes.

- Setting aggressive caching on immutable resources while using shorter cache durations for resources that change frequently.

- Employing service workers to programmatically manage caching for dynamic content and offline usage.

By understanding and applying the correct caching strategies, developers can significantly improve the performance of their web applications. Leveraging browser caching allows for reduced server load, faster page loads, and a better overall user experience.

5.7   Minification   and   Compression Techniques

Minification and compression are essential techniques in optimizing web applications' performance.   These processes dramatically reduce the size of code and asset files, leading to faster download times and improved user experience on web applications.   This discussion will focus on understanding these processes, the difference between them, and how they can be effectively applied in a Webpack build process.

Understanding Minification

Minification is the process of removing all unnecessary characters from source code without changing its functionality.   These characters include whitespace, newline characters, comments, and block delimiters, which are useful for human readability but superfluous for execution. The result is a significantly smaller file size, which translates to reduced bandwidth consumption and faster loading times.

To demonstrate minification, consider the following JavaScript code snippet:

```
1  function exampleFunction() {
2      // This is a comment
3      var x = "This is a string";
4      console.log(x);
5  }
```

After minification, the code would be transformed into:

```
function exampleFunction(){var x="This is a string";console.log(x);}
```

This condensed version removes the comment and unnecessary spaces, reducing the file size without affecting the code's execution.

Webpack integrates several plugins to automate the minification process. The `TerserWebpackPlugin` is one such plugin, optimized for JavaScript files. Configuration for this plugin can be specified as follows:

```
1  const TerserPlugin = require('terser-webpack-plugin');
2  module.exports = {
3      optimization: {
4          minimize: true,
5          minimizer: [new TerserPlugin({ /* options */ })],
6      },
7  };
```

Understanding Compression

Compression is another technique used to reduce file sizes, but it operates differently from minification. It involves encoding information using fewer bits than the original representation, making extensive use of algorithms to reduce file size. Compression can be of two types: lossless and lossy. Lossless compression reduces files sizes without losing any information, meaning the original data can be perfectly retrieved. Lossy compression, on the other hand, achieves greater size reduction at the cost of losing some data.

For web applications, lossless compression is widely used for text-based assets like CSS, HTML, and JavaScript, ensuring no loss in code quality or functionality. Gzip and Brotli are popular compression algorithms used in web development for this purpose.

Webpack facilitates asset compression through various plugins. For instance, to apply Brotli compression, one can use the `CompressionWebpackPlugin`:

```
1  const CompressionPlugin = require('compression-webpack-plugin');
```

```
2
3   module.exports = {
4       plugins: [
5           new CompressionPlugin({
6               filename: '[path].br[query]',
7               algorithm: 'brotliCompress',
8               test: /\.(js|css|html|svg)$/,
9               compressionOptions: { level: 11 },
10              threshold: 10240,
11              minRatio: 0.8,
12          }),
13      ],
14  };
```

Best Practices

To maximize the effectiveness of minification and compression, follow these best practices:

- Apply both techniques as part of your build process to complement each other for optimal size reduction.

- Use the latest versions of minification and compression tools to take advantage of performance improvements and new features.

- Configure compression to automatically exclude small files, as the overhead of compression may not yield a net benefit for them.

- Regularly audit your application's performance using tools like Webpack Bundle Analyzer to identify and address inefficiencies in your optimization strategies.

Implementing minification and compression as part of the Webpack build process is a straightforward and effective way to improve your web application's performance. By reducing the size of the assets that need to be downloaded, these techniques can significantly enhance the end-user experience, especially for those on slower internet connections or mobile devices.

5.8   Optimizing CSS Delivery

Optimizing the delivery of CSS is a fundamental aspect of improving the performance of web applications. CSS, being a critical resource, can block rendering until it is fully downloaded and parsed. Therefore, efficient delivery and loading of CSS are paramount in reducing perceived and actual load times, which enhances user experience. This section will detail strategies to optimize CSS delivery through various techniques, including critical CSS extraction, the use of media and attribute selectors, and applying asynchronous loading.

Critical CSS Extraction

Critical CSS refers to the minimal set of styling instructions required to render the visible portion of a web page, also known as the "above-the-fold" content. Extracting and inlining critical CSS directly into the HTML document can significantly reduce render-blocking time. The process involves identifying CSS rules that are essential for initial render and embedding those directly within the <head> tag of the HTML.

To automate the extraction of critical CSS, several tools can be utilized. One such tool is PurgeCSS, which analyzes your content and CSS files, removing unused selectors from your style sheets. Another tool, Critical, generates and inlines critical-path CSS. The integration of these tools in a Webpack build process can be achieved via respective plugins or loaders.

```
1  const PurgeCSSPlugin = require('purgecss-webpack-plugin');
2  const CriticalWebpackPlugin = require('critical-webpack-plugin');
3
4  // Webpack configuration
5  module.exports = {
6    // Other configurations omitted for brevity
7    plugins: [
8      new PurgeCSSPlugin({ /* options */ }),
9      new CriticalWebpackPlugin({ /* options */ }),
10   ],
11  };
```

135

Utilizing Media and Attribute Selectors

Media and attribute selectors allow developers to specify the conditions under which a set of CSS rules should be applied. This capability can be harnessed to defer the loading of non-critical styles, such as those applicable only for print media or specific device orientations.

```
1  <link rel="stylesheet" href="print.css" media="print">
2  <link rel="stylesheet" href="landscape.css" media="(orientation: landscape)">
```

By leveraging these selectors, browsers will only fetch these stylesheets when the specified conditions are met, thereby reducing unnecessary download and parsing of CSS not critical to the initial render.

Asynchronous Loading of CSS

Asynchronous loading of CSS can further enhance page load performance by non-blocking the download and processing of stylesheets. This technique involves loading CSS files asynchronously using JavaScript. However, this approach requires careful implementation to prevent FOUC (Flash of Unstyled Content).

One method to asynchronously load CSS is through the use of the rel="preload" attribute in a <link> tag, followed by dynamically setting the rel attribute to "stylesheet" using JavaScript, thereby applying the styles once loaded.

```
1  <link rel="preload" href="styles.css" as="style" onload="this.rel='stylesheet'">
2  <noscript><link rel="stylesheet" href="styles.css"></noscript>
```

The <noscript> tag ensures that the styles are still applied in environments where JavaScript is disabled, maintaining accessibility and functionality.

Optimizing CSS delivery is a multi-faceted approach that involves extracting critical CSS, leveraging media and attribute selectors to conditionally load styles, and applying asynchronous loading techniques. By implementing these strategies within a Webpack build process, developers can significantly enhance the loading speed and, consequently, the user experience of web applications.

5.9 Asset Management: Efficient Handling of Images and Fonts

Efficient asset management is essential in reducing the load time and improving the performance of web applications. This includes the optimal handling of images and fonts, which are often the heaviest parts of web applications. We will now discuss various techniques to manage these assets effectively.

Handling Images

Images play a crucial role in any web application but can significantly affect its performance if not handled properly. The following strategies can be employed to optimize image loading:

- **Image Compression:** Reducing the size of images without compromising their quality is the first step. Tools like `ImageOptim` and `TinyPNG` can achieve significant reductions.

- **Responsive Images:** Using the `<img srcset=`` ''>` attribute allows the browser to select the most appropriate image size based on the user's device, improving loading times and reducing data usage.

- **Using WebP Format:** WebP offers better compression than PNG and JPEG, without the loss of quality, reducing image sizes further.

- **Lazy Loading:** Images are loaded only when they enter the viewport, reducing initial load times. The `loading="lazy"` attribute on the `<img>` tag can be used to implement this.

Handling Fonts

Fonts, particularly web fonts, can also significantly impact web performance. The strategies below will help in their efficient handling:

- **Font Subsetting:** Many fonts include characters for multiple languages and symbols that your site may not use. Subsetting a font to include only the necessary characters can drastically reduce its size.

- **Using System Fonts:** System fonts load instantly because they are already installed on the user's device, eliminating the need to download any font files.

- **Font Loading Strategies:** CSS provides properties such as font-display: swap; to control how fonts are displayed. This property, in particular, uses the fallback font until the web font is fully loaded, improving the perceived performance.

Implementing Asset Optimization Techniques

Integration of these techniques into the Webpack environment requires the use of specific loaders and plugins. For images, image-webpack-loader can be used for compression, and for responsive images, responsive-loader fits well. To implement lazy loading, lozad.js or similar libraries can be integrated into your project.

For handling fonts, ensure that font files are correctly served with appropriate caching headers to minimize re-download times. When subsetting fonts, tools like Font Squirrel or glyphhanger can automate the process.

Here is an example of using the image-webpack-loader in your Webpack configuration:

```
1  module.exports = {
2      module: {
3          rules: [
4              {
```

```
5      test: /\.(png|svg|jpg|jpeg|gif)$/i,
6      use: [
7      {
8          loader: 'image-webpack-loader',
9          options: {
10         mozjpeg: {
11             progressive: true,
12         },
13         // Additional options can be specified here.
14         },
15     },
16     ],
17   },
18   ],
19   },
20 };
```

Following these asset management techniques ensures that your web applications load faster, offering a better user experience while conserving bandwidth. Making use of the latest web technologies and adhering to best practices in asset optimization can lead to substantial performance improvements.

5.10 Using Preloading and Prefetching

Preloading and prefetching are techniques designed to speed up the loading time of web applications by strategically managing resource loading priorities. Both approaches inform the browser about which resources are needed soon or later, allowing for a more intelligent use of network and idle times. However, they serve slightly different purposes and are implemented in distinct ways. Understanding the nuances between them is crucial for effective application performance optimization.

Preloading

Preloading is a technique used to inform the browser about critical resources that need to be loaded early in the page life cycle, even before the browser's engine discovers them while parsing the HTML. This is particularly useful for resources that are essential but are discovered late due to their location in the document or due to being called dynamically from scripts.

To implement preloading, the `<link rel="preload">` tag is used in the HTML document's head section. This instructs the browser to download the specified resource as soon as possible, without waiting for the parsing process to reveal its necessity. Preloading is especially advantageous for loading fonts, CSS files, and critical JavaScript bundles that are essential for the initial rendering of the page.

Example of preloading a font:

```
1  <link rel="preload" href="fonts/myFont.woff2" as="font" type="font/woff2"
       crossorigin>
```

Prefetching

Prefetching, on the other hand, is a technique aimed at loading resources that will be needed in the future. This method is more about predicting the resources that might be needed next and loading them during idle time. This ensures that when the user navigates to a new part of the application or a new page, the necessary resources are already in the cache, reducing load times significantly.

There are several types of prefetching, but the most common one is implemented using the `<link rel="prefetch">` tag. This tag, similar to preload, is placed in the HTML document but with resources that are not critical for the initial page load. Instead, these are resources that are likely needed for subsequent page loads or user actions.

Example of prefetching a JavaScript file:

```
1  <link rel="prefetch" href="js/nextPageScript.js">
```

Though preloading and prefetching are powerful tools for improving application performance, they should be used judiciously. Overuse can lead to bandwidth wastage and even slow down the application by competing for resources with critical assets.

It's vital to analyze your application's resource loading patterns and user interaction models to effectively leverage these techniques.

By strategically implementing preloading and prefetching, developers can optimize resource loading behavior, significantly improving the user experience by making web applications feel faster and more responsive.

5.11   Implementing HTTP/2 for Better Performance

Implementing HTTP/2 significantly enhances the performance of web applications by addressing many of the inefficiencies found in HTTP/1.x.   Unlike its predecessor, HTTP/2 introduces multiplexing, server push, header compression, and prioritization, making it a crucial optimization step in web development.

Multiplexing

Multiplexing is a core feature of HTTP/2 that allows multiple requests and responses to be in flight at the same time over a single TCP connection.   This process eliminates the need for multiple connections between the client and the server, reducing the overhead and latency associated with connection management. Here is an example demonstrating how to enable HTTP/2 in a Webpack development server:

```
const server = new WebpackDevServer(compiler, {
  http2: true,
  https: {
    key: fs.readFileSync("path/to/server.key"),
    cert: fs.readFileSync("path/to/server.crt")
  }
});
```

141

Server Push

Server push is another feature of HTTP/2, enabling the server to send resources to the client before the client specifically requests them. This preemptive sending can significantly reduce loading times by providing the client with resources it will need in advance. Configuring server push involves creating a link header. However, care must be taken to avoid pushing unnecessary resources, as this can increase bandwidth usage and negatively impact performance for clients with limited bandwidth.

Header Compression

HTTP/2 uses HPACK compression for headers, reducing the size of the headers that need to be transferred between the server and client. HPACK compression efficiently encodes headers, minimizing the overhead, especially in cases where similar headers are sent repeatedly in multiple requests. This feature of HTTP/2 doesn't require specific configuration in Webpack but is handled by the server supporting HTTP/2.

Prioritization

HTTP/2 allows the client to specify the priority of resources, enabling the server to deliver higher-priority resources faster. This prioritization ensures that critical resources are loaded first, improving the perceived performance of web applications. Implementing prioritization involves careful analysis and structuring of resource dependencies to align with the critical rendering path of the application.

Practical Tips for Implementation

When implementing HTTP/2, it is essential to ensure that the server and client support the protocol. Most modern browsers support HTTP/2, but server support must be explicitly enabled.

Additionally, since HTTP/2 runs over TLS in nearly all cases, obtaining and configuring a valid SSL/TLS certificate is necessary. Lastly, testing the configuration thoroughly to ensure all HTTP/2 features are working as expected is crucial for achieving the desired performance improvements.

Leveraging HTTP/2 is a powerful strategy for optimizing web application performance. By enabling multiplexing, server push, header compression, and prioritization, developers can significantly reduce latency, minimize resource loading times, and improve overall user experience. Implementing HTTP/2 requires careful planning and testing but can lead to substantial performance gains in modern web applications.

5.12 Optimization Best Practices and Common Pitfalls

Determining the most effective strategies for performance optimization demands a keen understanding of best practices alongside a familiarity with common pitfalls that can undermine efforts. These approaches apply to the utilization of Webpack for streamlining web applications.

Best Practices

- **Profile Before Optimizing**: Before implementing any optimization, use tools such as the Webpack Bundle Analyzer to understand where the actual bottlenecks are. Without data to support optimization efforts, time and resources may be wasted on unnecessary or ineffective adjustments.

- **Implement Code Splitting**: Splitting code into multiple chunks allows for loading only the necessary pieces for a given route or functionality, significantly reducing initial load times. Use the `import()` syntax for dynamic imports as a standard approach for code splitting in Webpack.

```
1    const HomePage = () => import('./HomePage');
```

- **Leverage Caching**: Configure your assets for long-term caching by employing content hashing in file names. Webpack's [contenthash] substitution ensures that file names are unique to the content.   This strategy prevents browsers from re-fetching unchanged assets, thereby decreasing load times on subsequent visits.

- **Utilize Tree Shaking**: Eliminate dead code from your bundles by enabling tree shaking, a process of removing unused code without affecting the functionality. Ensure that your project is using ES6 modules and that the sideEffects field in your package.json is correctly set to enable this feature.

- **Opt for Asset Compression**: Compress text-based assets using tools like Brotli or Gzip to reduce their size before they are sent over the network. This can be easily configured in Webpack through plugins such as CompressionWebpackPlugin.

Common Pitfalls

- **Over-Optimization**: Attempting to optimize everything all at once can lead to diminished returns. Focus on the biggest performance bottlenecks identified through profiling before addressing less critical areas.

- **Ignoring Browser Caching Potential**:   Failing to set up caching properly can result in browsers re-downloading assets unnecessarily.   Use hashing strategies and configure your server headers to maximize the caching capabilities of browsers.

- **Misconfiguring Code Splitting**: Improperly implemented code splitting can lead to worse performance if many small chunks are created, each requiring individual HTTP requests. Balance the size and number of chunks to optimize load times and minimize request overhead.

- **Exclusion of Tree Shaking**: By neglecting tree shaking or incorrectly configuring the `sideEffects` property, applications bundle and ship dead code, inflating the size unnecessarily. Ensure proper setup to take full advantage of this optimization feature.

- **Overlooking Modern JavaScript Syntax**: Older JavaScript syntax can prevent optimizations such as tree shaking from functioning correctly. Adopting modern ES6 syntax not only facilitates cleaner code but also enables more efficient bundling processes.

Implementing these best practices while avoiding common pitfalls empowers developers to significantly enhance the performance of their web applications. This balance requires a strategic approach to optimization, leveraging a deep understanding of Webpack's capabilities and how real-world factors influence web performance.

Chapter 6

Code Splitting and Lazy Loading

Code splitting and lazy loading are pivotal techniques in modern web development for reducing initial load times and improving application performance. This chapter delves into the mechanics of partitioning a codebase into various bundles that can be loaded on demand, thereby minimizing the amount of code processed during the initial load. It provides a thorough exploration of implementing these techniques in Webpack, including setting up dynamic imports and optimizing route-based code splitting in single-page applications. Real-world examples demonstrate how to strategically apply lazy loading to enhance user experience by prioritizing the content and features that users need most when they need them.

6.1   Introduction to Code Splitting and Its Benefits

Code splitting encompasses the strategy of breaking down a web application's codebase into smaller, manageable chunks that can be loaded as needed, rather than loading the entire application upfront. This method significantly improves initial load time, enhances user experience, and optimally utilizes bandwidth by loading only the necessary code at any point in time.

The core rationale behind code splitting lies in its ability to segregate the monolithic bundle of an application into distinct parts. Typically, a web application is packed into a single JavaScript file. However, not every function or module within that file is necessary from the outset. By dividing the application code into several bundles, only the essential initial code is loaded during the app's startup phase. The remaining code is fetched dynamically as the user interacts with the application, or when certain conditions are met.

In terms of benefits, code splitting and lazy loading provide numerous advantages:

- **Improved Load Time:** Since only a fraction of the code is loaded initially, the amount of data transferred over the network is substantially reduced, leading to faster application load times.

- **Reduced Resource Consumption:** Less code means less processing and, therefore, a lower consumption of computational resources on the client device. This is particularly advantageous for users with older hardware or slower internet connections.

- **Better User Experience:** By prioritizing the loading of content and features that are immediately necessary, users can start interacting with the application sooner, which contributes to a smoother and more engaging user experience.

- **Efficient Utilization of Cache:** Since the core application shell can be loaded separately from the content, updates to content do not necessitate the redownload of the application shell. This efficient cache strategy minimizes the amount of data users need to download when updates are made.

To implement code splitting in Webpack, a detailed understanding of various concepts and plugins is vital. Configuration adjustments facilitate the automatic division of the codebase into chunks through dynamic imports, the SplitChunksPlugin, and other relevant mechanisms offered by Webpack.

For instance, when employing dynamic imports in a JavaScript module, the syntax looks as follows:

```
import(/* webpackChunkName: "moduleName" */ 'path/to/module').then((module) => {
    // Operations to perform after module is loaded
});
```

This structure instructs Webpack to separate the specified module from the main bundle, assign it a name for easier identification, and load it only when needed. The resulting separation is crucial for optimizing the application's loading performance.

Similarly, the SplitChunksPlugin automatically identifies modules that can be shared between chunks and splits them off into their own bundles, thus preventing redundancy and enhancing efficiency. Configuring this plugin correctly is essential for maximizing the potential of code splitting.

In summary, code splitting and lazy loading are indispensable techniques in the modern web development toolkit, offering significant improvements in performance, user experience, and resource management. Through the strategic application of these methods, developers can build web applications that are not only faster and more responsive but also more scalable and maintainable.

6.2   Configuring Webpack for Code Splitting

Configuring Webpack to enable code splitting involves several key steps aimed at optimizing the build process to create separate bundles. Code splitting is a strategy that segregates code into various bundles which are loaded on demand, dramatically decreasing the initial load time and improving the performance of web applications. This section will walk through the essential configurations needed to implement code splitting in Webpack.

First, it is important to understand the role of the entry point in Webpack configuration. The entry point is the starting point for Webpack to begin its process of building the dependency graph and subsequently creating bundles. To facilitate code splitting, multiple entry points can be defined, or dynamic imports can be used within a single entry point application.

```
1  module.exports = {
2    entry: {
3      main: './src/index.js',
4      vendor: './src/vendor.js'
5    }
6  };
```

The above configuration demonstrates how to define multiple entry points. Here, 'main' and 'vendor' are separate entry points that will result in different output bundles. This is a manual way of splitting code that requires explicit definition of each bundle's contents.

Moving forward, Webpack provides an optimization feature known as SplitChunksPlugin, which automates the splitting of code. It is particularly useful for identifying common dependencies between chunks and separating them into shared bundles. The SplitChunksPlugin is enabled by default in Webpack 4 and above; however, its behavior can be customized through various options in the Webpack configuration file.

```
1  module.exports = {
2    optimization: {
3      splitChunks: {
4        chunks: 'all',
5        minSize: 20000,
6        maxSize: 0,
```

```
7    minChunks: 1,
8    maxAsyncRequests: 6,
9    maxInitialRequests: 4,
10   automaticNameDelimiter: '~',
11   cacheGroups: {
12     defaultVendors: {
13       test: /[\\/]node_modules[\\/]/,
14       priority: -10
15     },
16     default: {
17       minChunks: 2,
18       priority: -20,
19       reuseExistingChunk: true
20     }
21   }
22  }
23  }
24 };
```

The 'splitChunks' option is where the configuration for the SplitChunksPlugin is set. The example configuration above specifies that chunks can be shared between asynchronous and non-asynchronous chunks ('chunks: 'all''). Parameters such as 'minSize', 'maxSize', and 'minChunks' dictate the conditions under which splitting occurs. The 'cacheGroups' option allows the grouping of chunks into common bundles based on the conditions specified.

Dynamic imports represent another approach to code splitting by allowing parts of your code to be loaded on demand. JavaScript supports dynamic imports that Webpack leverages to split code automatically.

```
1  import(/* webpackChunkName: "utility" */ './utility.js').then((module) => {
2    let utility = module.default;
3    console.log(utility);
4  });
```

In the example above, the 'webpackChunkName' comment tells Webpack to name the output chunk "utility". This code will cause 'utility.js' and its dependencies to be split into a separate chunk that is only loaded when the import statement is executed.

Lastly, it is critical to ensure that the output configuration in Webpack is set to handle multiple bundles efficiently by including placeholders such as '[name]' or '[chunkhash]' in the filename template.

```
1  module.exports = {
2    output: {
3      filename: '[name].[contenthash].bundle.js',
4      path: __dirname + '/dist'
5    }
6  };
```

Using '[contenthash]' in the filename ensures that browsers cache each bundle properly and only download them again when their contents change. This configuration will output each bundle with a name and content hash, facilitating cache management and avoiding unnecessary downloads by the user's browser.

Code splitting in Webpack is facilitated through a variety of configurations and techniques. Whether using multiple entry points, the SplitChunksPlugin, or dynamic imports, Webpack provides a flexible base for segmenting application code into smaller, more manageable bundles. Through these mechanisms, developers can significantly enhance the performance of web applications by reducing the initial load time and making resources available on-demand.

6.3   Using SplitChunksPlugin for Vendor and Common Chunks

Webpack's SplitChunksPlugin is a built-in feature purpose-built for optimizing the bundling process by identifying common modules shared between chunk and splitting those out into separate bundles. This can significantly reduce the size of the chunks that need to be loaded initially, which in turn can impact the page's load time positively. The focus of this section is to understand how to utilize the SplitChunksPlugin for extracting vendor and common chunks effectively.

The primary configuration for SplitChunksPlugin can be found in the optimization.splitChunks section of your Webpack configuration file. Its default settings are often adequate for many projects, but understanding and fine-tuning the configuration can lead to more optimized bundling.

```
module.exports = {
  //...
  optimization: {
    splitChunks: {
      chunks: 'all',
      minSize: 20000,
      minRemainingSize: 0,
      maxSize: 0,
      minChunks: 1,
      maxAsyncRequests: 30,
      maxInitialRequests: 30,
      enforceSizeThreshold: 50000,
      cacheGroups: {
        defaultVendors: {
          test: /[\\/]node_modules[\\/]/,
          priority: -10,
          reuseExistingChunk: true,
        },
        default: {
          minChunks: 2,
          priority: -20,
          reuseExistingChunk: true
        },
      },
    },
  },
};
```

The configuration above instructs Webpack to apply the chunk splitting strategy to all chunks (chunks: 'all') and defines rules for the creation of vendor and common chunks within the cacheGroups property. The defaultVendors group targets modules located in the node_modules directory, typically third-party libraries, and separates them into a vendors chunk. The default group, on the other hand, is designed to capture common modules that appear in at least two chunks, consolidating them into a common chunk.

Let's dissect the key configurations:

- chunks: 'all' enables the splitting for all types of chunks (async and non-async). This is essential for achieving a comprehensive code splitting strategy.

- minSize specifies the minimum size, in bytes, for a chunk to be generated. It helps in avoiding the creation of overly small chunks.

- `minChunks` indicates the minimum number of chunks that must share a module before it's split out. Setting this to 2 ensures that only the modules used in multiple places are extracted.

- `cacheGroups` allows defining specific conditions for groupings of modules into chunks. This is where you precisely control how the vendor and common chunks are created.

When Webpack processes your application with this configuration, it generates separate chunks for vendor and common modules, effectively reducing the initial load time by only loading what's necessary and caching the rest for future requests.

By adjusting these configurations, developers have fine-grained control over the chunk splitting behavior, enabling them to tailor the bundling process to the specific needs of their application for optimal performance.

Additionally, it's worthwhile to mention that careful observation and analysis of the output bundles using Webpack's bundle analysis tools can provide insights into further optimizations. Iteratively refining the SplitChunksPlugin configuration based on real-world usage patterns and bundle analysis findings can lead to significant performance improvements over time.

6.4   Dynamic Imports in JavaScript for Lazy Loading

Dynamic imports in JavaScript are a critical feature that enables developers to implement lazy loading in web applications efficiently. This technique allows modules to be loaded dynamically at runtime, instead of at the initial page load, which can significantly reduce the amount of JavaScript that needs to be downloaded, parsed, and executed upfront. This section will focus on how dynamic imports work, how to use them for lazy loading, and the best practices to optimize their usage.

A dynamic import in JavaScript is expressed as a function-like form of the 'import' statement which returns a promise. This promise resolves into a module object that contains all the exports from the imported module. The syntax for dynamic import is as shown below:

```
1  import("path/to/module")
2      .then(module => {
3          // Use module
4      })
5      .catch(error => {
6          // Handle error
7      });
```

This promise-based approach makes dynamic imports naturally fit for use cases where modules need to be loaded on demand. For instance, when a user interacts with a part of an application that requires additional, not initially loaded, JavaScript functionality.

Consider a web application that includes a complex charting functionality which is only needed when navigating to a specific section of the application. Traditionally, the entire charting library would be included in the main JavaScript bundle, increasing the initial load time. However, using dynamic imports, the charting library can be loaded only when the user accesses that specific section. Here is how this can be implemented:

```
1  button.addEventListener('click', () => {
2      import("./path/to/charting-library")
3          .then(chartingLibrary => {
4              chartingLibrary.renderChart(container);
5          })
6          .catch(error => {
7              console.error("Failed to load charting library", error);
8          });
9  });
```

When implementing dynamic imports for lazy loading, several best practices should be considered to maximize their effectiveness:

- Use dynamic imports for large modules that are not immediately needed. This includes third-party libraries, heavy assets, and feature-specific code.

155

- Preload important modules that are likely to be needed soon after the initial load but are not critical for the initial rendering. This can be achieved using the `<link rel="preload">` hint in HTML.

- Provide feedback to users when loading modules dynamically, especially if it might take some time. Implementing loading indicators or placeholders can improve the user experience.

- Test and monitor the performance impact of dynamic imports. Tools such as Webpack's Bundle Analyzer can help identify the best candidates for dynamic imports and evaluate the impact on the application's load time.

Furthermore, error handling plays an essential role when working with dynamic imports. Since loading a module dynamically involves network requests, it introduces the possibility of failure due to network issues or the requested module being unavailable. Proper error handling ensures that the application can gracefully handle such scenarios, perhaps by retrying the import or displaying a user-friendly error message.

```
1  import("./path/to/module")
2    .then(module => {
3        // Module loaded successfully
4    })
5    .catch(error => {
6        // Handle loading error
7        console.error("Module failed to load", error);
8    });
```

Dynamic imports in JavaScript are a powerful feature that facilitates lazy loading, enabling developers to improve their web application's performance significantly. By understanding how to effectively use dynamic imports and by following best practices for their implementation, developers can ensure that their applications are both performant and user-friendly.

6.5 Lazy Loading React Components with React.lazy and Suspense

To achieve an optimal user experience in single-page applications (SPAs) developed with React, leveraging lazy loading for components is a critical strategy. This technique ensures that components are loaded only when they are needed, thereby reducing the bundle size loaded during the application's initial startup. React provides built-in support for lazy loading through two key features: 'React.lazy' and 'Suspense'.

Implementing React.lazy

'React.lazy' is a function that enables you to render a dynamic import as a regular component. This functionality allows the component to be loaded only when it is required, rather than at the startup of the application. The syntax for using 'React.lazy' is straightforward and involves passing a function that calls a dynamic 'import()' statement, which returns a 'Promise' that resolves to a module containing a React component.

```
import React, { lazy, Suspense } from 'react';

const LazyLoadedComponent = lazy(() => import('./LazyLoadedComponent'));

function App() {
  return (
    <div>
      <Suspense fallback={<div>Loading...</div>}>
        <LazyLoadedComponent />
      </Suspense>
    </div>
  );
}

export default App;
```

In the example above, 'LazyLoadedComponent' will only be loaded when the 'App' component renders it for the first time. Until the component is loaded, the 'fallback' prop of 'Suspense' provides a temporary UI element to display, such as a loading indicator.

Utilizing Suspense

'Suspense' is a React component that wraps lazy-loaded components. It allows you to specify the loading state UI for any component or group of components that are being loaded lazily. The 'fallback' prop accepts any React elements that you want to render while waiting for the lazy component to be loaded. It is possible to use multiple 'Suspense' components in different parts of your application to display different loading states for different sections of your UI.

```
const OtherComponent = lazy(() => import('./OtherComponent'));
const AnotherComponent = lazy(() => import('./AnotherComponent'));

function App() {
  return (
    <div>
      <Suspense fallback={<div>Loading component...</div>}>
        <OtherComponent />
      </Suspense>
      <Suspense fallback={<div>Loading another component...</div>}>
        <AnotherComponent />
      </Suspense>
    </div>
  );
}
```

Error Boundaries with Suspense and Lazy Loading

When implementing lazy loading with 'React.lazy' and 'Suspense', it is important to handle errors that may occur during the loading of a component. This is particularly crucial for ensuring a seamless user experience when network issues or other errors prevent a component from loading successfully. React recommends using error boundaries in conjunction with 'Suspense' to catch and handle these errors gracefully.

An error boundary is a React component that catches JavaScript errors anywhere in their child component tree, logs those errors, and displays a fallback UI instead of the component tree that crashed. Error boundaries do not catch errors for:

- Event handlers

- Asynchronous   code   (e.g.,   'setTimeout'   or
  'requestAnimationFrame' callbacks)

- Server-side rendering

- Errors thrown in the error boundary itself (rather than its children)

To create an error boundary, declare a new class component that extends 'React.Component' and implement the 'static getDerivedStateFromError()' or the 'componentDidCatch()' lifecycle methods.

```
import React, { Component } from 'react';

class ErrorBoundary extends Component {
  constructor(props) {
    super(props);
    this.state = { hasError: false };
  }

  static getDerivedStateFromError(error) {
    // Update state so the next render will show the fallback UI.
    return { hasError: true };
  }

  componentDidCatch(error, errorInfo) {
    // You can also log the error to an error reporting service
    logErrorToMyService(error, errorInfo);
  }

  render() {
    if (this.state.hasError) {
      // You can render any custom fallback UI
      return <h1>Something went wrong.</h1>;
    }

    return this.props.children;
  }
}
```

With an error boundary in place, you can wrap your 'Suspense' and lazy-loaded components to handle any errors gracefully, ensuring that your application remains robust and user-friendly under various circumstances.

6.6   Integrating Lazy Loading with Vue.js

Integrating lazy loading in Vue.js applications significantly improves performance by loading components on-demand, rather than at the initial loading. Vue provides built-in support for lazy loading, especially beneficial in applications that have a large number of components leading to large bundle sizes. This section covers the integration process, utilizing Vue's dynamic import feature alongside webpack's code splitting capabilities.

To begin, let's consider a Vue application that has multiple routes, each corresponding to a different component. In a conventional setup, webpack bundles all these components together during the build process, resulting in a large bundle that the user must download when first visiting the application. By implementing lazy loading, each component is loaded only when the user navigates to the corresponding route, hence reducing the initial load time.

The core principle of implementing lazy loading in Vue.js revolves around dynamic imports. Dynamic imports are a JavaScript feature that allows modules to be loaded on-demand. When used with Vue.js and webpack, dynamic imports enable splitting the bundle into smaller chunks, each associated with a particular route or component.

Let's look at an example of converting a regular import to a dynamic import in a Vue application's router configuration:

```
1  // Before: Regular import
2  import HomePage from './components/HomePage.vue';
3
4  // After: Dynamic import
5  const HomePage = () => import('./components/HomePage.vue');
```

In the example above, the regular import is replaced with a dynamic import within a function. This function returns a promise resolving to the component, indicating that the component is loaded only when the function is invoked, i.e., when the route is accessed.

For more intricate scenarios, Vue's async components can be paired with webpack's magic comments to achieve more refined control over chunk naming and prefetching behavior. Magic comments are special syntax in webpack that provides additional instructions during the bundle generation process. They can specify chunk names, instruct webpack to prefetch or preload chunks, among other things. Here's how to use them with dynamic imports:

```
1  const AboutPage = () => import(/* webpackChunkName: "about" */ './
       components/AboutPage.vue');
```

The webpackChunkName directive in the comment specifies a name for the chunk associated with the AboutPage component. This name appears in the generated bundle, making it easier to identify and analyze the chunk during debugging and optimization.

Vue also provides the <router-link> component with v-bind directives to seamlessly integrate lazy loading in applications that use Vue Router for navigation. By combining dynamic imports with Vue Router's lazy loading capabilities, developers can drastically reduce initial load times, enhancing the user experience.

To ensure that lazy-loaded components provide feedback while they are being loaded, Vue recommends using component-level indicators such as loaders or placeholders. This can be handled elegantly in Vue by utilizing the component's asynchronous import along with its loading, error, and delay properties to manage the loading state.

In summary, integrating lazy loading in Vue.js applications leveraging webpack's code splitting feature and Vue's support for dynamic imports and async components greatly improves application performance. It reduces initial load times, enhances user experience by loading only what is necessary when it's necessary, and provides developers with powerful tools to optimize their applications effectively.

6.7   Optimizing Angular Applications with Module Federation

Optimizing Angular applications necessitates leveraging advanced techniques like Module Federation, which facilitates the architecture of micro frontends in a seamless and efficient manner. This approach is paramount for splitting a large-scale Angular application into smaller, manageable, independently deployable chunks. Module Federation allows these chunks, or "modules", to share dependencies and communicate with each other at runtime, significantly enhancing the application's scalability and maintainability while optimally utilizing web resources.

To implement Module Federation in Angular applications, certain core steps need to be meticulously adhered to, ensuring that both the host and remote applications are correctly configured.

Setting up the Host Application

The host application is the main entry point for users. It is responsible for dynamically loading remote modules (micro frontends) when needed. Begin by configuring the Webpack module federation plugin in the `webpack.config.js` file of the host application:

```
1   const ModuleFederationPlugin = require("webpack/lib/container/
        ModuleFederationPlugin");
2
3   module.exports = {
4     plugins: [
5       new ModuleFederationPlugin({
6         name: "host",
7         remotes: {
8           remoteApp: "remoteApp@http://localhost:3001/remoteEntry.js"
9         },
10        shared: ["@angular/core", "@angular/common", "@angular/router"]
11      }),
12    ],
13  };
```

The name field specifies the name of the host application. The remotes field is an object that maps remote applications to their entry points. shared lists all common dependencies that should not be duplicated if they are also used by remote modules.

Configuring the Remote Application

The configuration of the remote application is similar but focuses on exposing its modules to the host application. Modify its webpack.config.js as follows:

```
1  const ModuleFederationPlugin = require("webpack/lib/container/
       ModuleFederationPlugin");
2
3  module.exports = {
4    plugins: [
5      new ModuleFederationPlugin({
6        name: "remoteApp",
7        filename: "remoteEntry.js",
8        exposes: {
9          './Module': './src/app/modules/some-module/some-module.module.ts',
10         },
11         shared: ["@angular/core", "@angular/common", "@angular/router"]
12       }),
13     ],
14   };
```

Here, the name identifies the remote application. The filename specifies the name of the bundle that the host will load. The exposes field lists the modules that are exposed for the host to consume, with key/-value pairs representing alias paths and actual file locations, respectively.

Integrating Federated Modules into the Host Application

To load and use a module from the remote application, the host application must dynamically import it:

```
1  loadRemoteModule() {
2    import('remoteApp/Module')
3      .then((remoteModule) => {
4        // Use the federated module
5      })
6      .catch(err => console.error("Error loading remote module", err));
7  }
```

By calling `loadRemoteModule`, the host application dynamically imports the module exposed by the remote application, using the alias defined in the remote application's `webpack.config.js` file.

Optimizing Shared Dependencies

To further optimize the application, it is crucial to pay attention to the `shared` configuration in both the host and remote applications. This ensures that common libraries are not loaded multiple times, reducing the overall bundle size and load time. Webpack takes care of version discrepancies as long as compatible versions are specified.

Adopting Module Federation in Angular applications introduces a scalable architecture that not only enhances performance through optimized bundle sizes but also improves the development process by enabling a micro-frontend approach. Proper configuration of the host and remote applications, along with careful management of shared dependencies, are essential steps in leveraging the full potential of Module Federation.   This modern technique undoubtedly catalyzes the evolution of web development, promoting more efficient and modular applications.

6.8   Strategies for Effective Code Splitting

To harness the full benefits of code splitting, strategic planning and execution are paramount. It's not merely about dividing code but doing so in a way that optimally enhances performance without compromising the integrity or maintainability of the codebase. This section will discuss various strategies to achieve effective code splitting, focusing on identifying split points, leveraging dynamic imports, and employing route-based code splitting.

Identifying Split Points

The first step in implementing code splitting is identifying the appropriate points in the application where the code can be split. These points are often modules or components that are not required during the initial load but might be needed later as the user interacts with the application. A meticulous approach is required to determine these points to ensure that the splitting aligns with user behavior patterns and application architecture.

- **Entry Points:** Consider splitting at the entry points of the application. For single-page applications (SPAs), this could mean different pages represented by components or modules.

- **User Flow:** Analyze the user flow within your application. Areas of the app that are accessed less frequently present good opportunities for code splitting.

- **Heavy Libraries or Modules:** Any heavyweight libraries or modules that are not essential for the initial rendering should be considered for splitting to improve the initial load time.

Leveraging Dynamic Imports

Dynamic imports are a cornerstone in achieving code splitting by allowing sections of code to be loaded only when they are needed. This is contrary to static imports, which load all modules at startup, regardless of whether they are immediately used. Dynamic imports can be introduced in your codebase as follows:

```
1  if (condition) {
2      import('path/to/module').then((module) => {
3          // Use module here
4      });
5  }
```

In the snippet above, the module is only loaded if the specified condition is true, thereby reducing the initial load time. This technique is particularly effective when applied judiciously across your application, focusing on large modules or components that are used conditionally or in response to user actions.

Route-Based Code Splitting for SPAs

For single-page applications, route-based code splitting is an effective strategy to enhance performance. Each route generally corresponds to a different view or component, and since a user is only interacting with one view at a time, there is no need to load all views upfront.

Configuring route-based code splitting can be done using dynamic imports combined with the router configuration in your web application:

```
// Example using React Router
import React, {lazy} from 'react';
import {BrowserRouter as Router, Route, Switch} from 'react-router-dom';

const Home = lazy(() => import('./Home'));
const About = lazy(() => import('./About'));

const App = () => (
   <Router>
      <Suspense fallback={<div>Loading...</div>}>
         <Switch>
            <Route exact path="/" component={Home} />
            <Route path="/about" component={About} />
         </Switch>
      </Suspense>
   </Router>
);
```

In the example above, 'React.lazy' and 'Suspense' are used to dynamically load the 'Home' and 'About' components based on the route, ensuring that the code for each view is loaded only when needed.

Effective code splitting is more art than science, requiring a deep understanding of the application structure and user behavior. By judiciously applying the strategies outlined above—identifying split points, leveraging dynamic imports, and employing route-based splitting—developers can significantly enhance application performance. This involves careful planning and repeated testing to identify the best split points and to ensure that the benefits of reduced initial load times are realized without negatively impacting the overall user experience.

6.9 Lazy Loaded Routes in Single Page Applications

Implementing lazy loading for routes in single-page applications (SPAs) is a technique that significantly enhances performance by loading components only when they're needed by the user. This approach is particularly effective in SPAs, where the browser does not refresh the whole page but dynamically updates the content as users interact with the application. This section will discuss the methodology for implementing lazy-loaded routes in different JavaScript frameworks, focusing on React, Vue.js, and Angular.

React: Using React.lazy and React Router

React provides a built-in mechanism for code splitting and lazy loading through the 'React.lazy' function. When integrating it with React Router, it allows for the dynamic loading of components for given routes. Here's how you can implement it:

```
import React, { Suspense, lazy } from 'react';
import { BrowserRouter as Router, Route, Switch } from 'react-router-dom';

const HomePage = lazy(() => import('./HomePage'));
const AboutPage = lazy(() => import('./AboutPage'));

function App() {
  return (
    <Router>
      <Suspense fallback={<div>Loading...</div>}>
        <Switch>
          <Route exact path="/" component={HomePage} />
          <Route path="/about" component={AboutPage} />
        </Switch>
      </Suspense>
    </Router>
  );
}
```

In the example above, 'React.lazy' is used to dynamically import the 'HomePage' and 'AboutPage' components. The 'Suspense' component wraps the route definitions and specifies a fallback UI to display while the lazy-loaded component is being fetched.

Vue.js: Async Components and Vue Router

Vue.js allows for lazy loading routes in conjunction with the Vue Router by defining components as asynchronous functions. The process is straightforward:

```
1   import Vue from 'vue';
2   import Router from 'vue-router';
3
4   Vue.use(Router);
5
6   export default new Router({
7     routes: [
8       {
9         path: '/',
10        name: 'home',
11        component: () => import('./views/HomePage.vue')
12      },
13      {
14        path: '/about',
15        name: 'about',
16        component: () => import('./views/AboutPage.vue')
17      }
18    ]
19  });
```

In this setup, the 'import' statement within the component declaration for each route instructs Vue Router to load the component asynchronously.

Angular: Route-based Lazy Loading

Angular provides a powerful and straightforward way to implement lazy-loaded routes using the Angular Router. This technique involves creating feature modules and declaring them in the routing configuration with the 'loadChildren' method.

```
1   const routes: Routes = [
2     {
```

```
 3      path: 'home',
 4      loadChildren: () => import('./home/home.module').then(m => m.HomeModule)
 5    },
 6    {
 7      path: 'about',
 8      loadChildren: () => import('./about/about.module').then(m => m.AboutModule)
 9    }
10  ];
11
12  @NgModule({
13    imports: [RouterModule.forRoot(routes)],
14    exports: [RouterModule]
15  })
16  export class AppRoutingModule { }
```

In the Angular example above, each route specifies a module to be lazily loaded when the route is activated. The 'loadChildren' attribute takes a function that dynamically imports the desired module.

Benefits of Lazy Loaded Routes

Implementing lazy loading for routes offers several benefits:

- Reduced initial load time: Since code is loaded on demand, the amount of code required to be transferred and parsed during the initial load is significantly decreased.

- Improved performance: Loading the essential code when it's needed can lead to a smoother user experience and faster application performance.

- Better resource utilization: Lazy loading helps in utilizing bandwidth and processing resources more effectively by avoiding the download of unnecessary code.

Lazy-loaded routes in SPAs play a crucial role in enhancing the application's performance and user experience by optimizing the load times and resource utilization. Properly implementing this technique, in correlation with the specific frameworks' best practices, can lead to significant improvements in application efficiency.

6.10   Improving User Experience with Lazy Loading

Improving user experience (UX) is a fundamental goal in web development. Lazy loading, a strategy that delays the loading of non-critical resources at page load time, directly contributes to this objective. By implementing lazy loading, developers can significantly reduce initial load time, decrease network traffic, and improve the responsiveness of a web application.

To understand the impact of lazy loading on UX, consider the user's perception of speed. A key metric here is the First Contentful Paint (FCP), which measures the time from navigation to the moment when the browser renders the first bit of content from the DOM. Another vital metric is the Time to Interactive (TTI), the time it takes for a page to become fully interactive. Lazy loading can positively affect both metrics by reducing the amount of code and resources that need to be loaded and processed before the page can render content and become interactive.

The implementation of lazy loading typically involves the following steps:

- Identifying the non-critical resources or components that can be loaded lazily.

- Using dynamic imports in JavaScript to split the codebase into multiple chunks.

- Implementing placeholders or skeleton screens that are shown while the lazy-loaded components are being fetched.

Dynamic imports in JavaScript are a cornerstone of lazy loading. They allow developers to import modules on demand, splitting the codebase into smaller, manageable chunks. Consider the following example where dynamic import is used to lazy load a component:

```
1  // Dynamic import statement
2  import('path/to/component').then((Component) => {
```

```
3      // Use the imported component
4   });
```

When a user navigates to a part of the application that requires this component, the import is triggered, and the component is fetched and loaded into the browser. This is in contrast to the traditional model, where all scripts are loaded upfront, regardless of whether they are immediately needed.

To further illustrate the benefits of lazy loading, consider a case where a media-heavy page includes high-resolution images or videos. These resources significantly contribute to the page's weight and loading time. By applying lazy loading to these media resources, they are only loaded when they enter the viewport or when the user interacts with them. This approach can be implemented using the Intersection Observer API or third-party libraries designed for this purpose.

```
1   let options = {
2       root: null,
3       rootMargin: '0px',
4       threshold: 0.1
5   };
6
7   let observer = new IntersectionObserver(handleIntersect, options);
8
9   function handleIntersect(entries, observer) {
10      entries.forEach(entry => {
11          if (entry.isIntersecting) {
12              // Load the image or video
13              entry.target.src = entry.target.dataset.src;
14              observer.unobserve(entry.target);
15          }
16      });
17  }
18
19  document.querySelectorAll('img.lazy').forEach(img => {
20      observer.observe(img);
21  });
```

In this example, the Intersection Observer API is used to observe images with the class 'lazy'. When these images come into view, their source attribute is updated to the actual image URL, triggering the browser to load them.

Lazy loading is a powerful technique for improving the user experience of web applications. It optimizes resource loading, which can significantly enhance the perceived and actual performance of a web page. While implementing lazy loading requires consideration of which components and resources to defer and understanding the technical mechanisms, the benefits in terms of improved speed and responsiveness are undeniable.

6.11   Debugging Code Splitting Issues

Debugging code splitting issues in Webpack can sometimes be a complex task due to the asynchronous nature of loading modules. However, understanding common pitfalls and effective debugging strategies can significantly simplify the process.

When code splitting does not function as expected, the reasons can be multifaceted, ranging from misconfigurations in the Webpack setup to incorrect usage of dynamic imports. To systematically approach these issues, follow the outlined steps and guidelines below.

- **Verify Webpack Configuration**: Ensure that your Webpack configuration is set up correctly for code splitting. Specifically, look into the `optimization.splitChunks` settings, as misconfigurations here are a common source of issues.

- **Check Dynamic Imports**: Dynamic imports are pivotal for lazy loading modules. Verify that the syntax used for dynamic imports is correct and consistent throughout your application. Use the `import()` function, and make sure that it is being called as expected.

```
1    // Correct use of dynamic import
2    import(`./modules/${moduleName}`).then(module => {
3        // Use the dynamically imported module
4        module.doSomething();
5    }).catch(error => {
6        console.error(`Error loading ${moduleName}:`, error);
7    });
```

- **Analyzing Bundle Output**: Webpack generates bundle files that can be inspected to understand how the code has been split. Tools like Webpack Bundle Analyzer can visualize the composition of your bundles, showing which modules are included in each. If unexpected dependencies are bundled together, it can be indicative of an issue with your split criteria.

- **Inspect Network Requests in Developer Tools**: Use the Network tab in your browser's developer tools to monitor the loading of bundle files. Bundle files that are not being loaded as expected might indicate incorrect paths or issues with the server configuration. There should be distinct network requests for each async-loaded chunk.

- **Test Lazy Loaded Routes**: For applications using route-based code splitting, ensure that routes are correctly triggering the loading of associated component chunks. Any delay or failure to load might indicate an issue with route definitions or dynamic import statements.

- **Logging and Error Handling in Dynamic Imports**: Incorporate logging and error handling within the promise returned by the dynamic import() to catch and diagnose any issues that occur during the loading of modules.

```
1  import(`./dynamicModules/${moduleName}`).then(module => {
2      console.log(`${moduleName} loaded successfully`);
3  }).catch(error => {
4      console.error(`Failed to load ${moduleName}:`, error);
5  });
```

- **Update Webpack and Plugins**: Ensure that you are using the latest versions of Webpack and related plugins. Sometimes, bugs affecting code splitting are resolved in newer versions.

Remember, debugging is a process of elimination. By methodically going through these steps and closely examining the output and behavior of your application, you will be able to identify and rectify the issues hindering effective code splitting in your Webpack configuration.

6.12 Best Practices for Code Splitting and Lazy Loading

Code splitting and lazy loading are powerful strategies for optimizing web applications. When utilized correctly, they lead to faster loading times and a smoother user experience. However, to achieve the best results, it's crucial to follow a set of best practices. This section will cover the most effective techniques for implementing code splitting and lazy loading within your projects.

Identify Split Points Strategically

When implementing code splitting, it's essential to identify the most effective points in your application to introduce splits. Common approaches include:

- Splitting at route level: This is particularly effective in single-page applications (SPAs) where different routes can load different components or modules lazily.

- Component-level splitting: Useful for large components that are not immediately required on the initial load.

- Library or vendor splitting: External libraries or frequently used utilities can be split into separate chunks to cache them effectively across different parts of your application.

Identifying these split points requires understanding your application's structure and how users interact with it.

Optimize Your Webpack Configuration

To implement code splitting in Webpack, certain optimizations can be applied to your configuration file:

```
1  module.exports = {
2     optimization: {
```

174

```
3    splitChunks: {
4      chunks: 'all',
5    },
6  },
7  };
```

This configuration uses the `SplitChunksPlugin` to automatically split vendor and common code across all chunks. It is a starting point and can be further customized based on the specific needs of your application.

Leverage Dynamic Imports for Lazy Loading

Dynamic imports in JavaScript allow you to import modules only when they are needed, making them a cornerstone for lazy loading:

```
1  button.onclick = () => {
2    import('./module.js')
3      .then(module => {
4        module.loadFunction();
5      })
6      .catch(err => {
7        console.log(err.message);
8      });
9  };
```

This code snippet demonstrates triggering a module load ('module.js') dynamically when a button is clicked, rather than at the initial script evaluation.

Use React.lazy and Suspense for React Applications

For React applications, leveraging 'React.lazy' and 'Suspense' simplifies the process of code splitting and lazy loading:

```
1   import React, { Suspense, lazy } from 'react';
2   const LazyComponent = lazy(() => import('./LazyComponent'));
3
4   function MyComponent() {
5     return (
6       <Suspense fallback={<div>Loading...</div>}>
7         <LazyComponent />
8       </Suspense>
9     );
10  }
```

This snippet shows how to lazily load a React component ('LazyComponent') with a fallback UI displayed while the component is loading.

Monitor and Measure Performance

After implementing code splitting and lazy loading, it's vital to monitor and measure the performance improvements using tools such as Google's Lighthouse or Webpack's Bundle Analyzer. These tools help identify further optimization opportunities and ensure that the implementations have positively impacted the application's load time and overall performance.

Continuous Refinement

Code splitting and lazy loading strategies should not be set-and-forget. They require continuous refinements as the application evolves. Regularly revisiting the split points, analyzing user flow, and assessing new features or routes are essential for maintaining optimal performance.

By adopting these best practices, developers can maximize the benefits of code splitting and lazy loading, leading to enhanced application performance and a better end-user experience.

Chapter 7

Webpack and CSS: Styles and Preprocessors

This chapter addresses the integral process of incorporating CSS and its preprocessors into a Webpack build, ensuring styles are efficiently managed and applied. It delves into the configuration of loaders such as css-loader and style-loader, and the use of preprocessors like SASS, LESS, and Stylus to enhance CSS capabilities. Furthermore, the chapter explores strategies for optimizing CSS delivery, such as extracting CSS into separate files, purging unused CSS, and implementing critical CSS. Through practical guidance and examples, readers will gain the skills to effectively manage styles within their Webpack-configured projects, resulting in cleaner code and improved performance.

7.1 Configuring   Webpack   for   CSS Processing

Webpack, serving as a powerful tool for bundling JavaScript, can also be configured to process other types of files like CSS. To handle CSS effectively, Webpack relies on specific loaders that enable it to recognize and bundle CSS files along with JavaScript, thereby streamlining the entire development workflow.

Let's start with the basics of configuring loaders in the Webpack configuration file. For CSS processing, two main loaders are essential: `css-loader` and `style-loader`. The `css-loader` interprets `@import` and `url()` like import/require() and will resolve them. On the other hand, the `style-loader` injects CSS into the DOM.

```
 1   module.exports = {
 2     module: {
 3       rules: [
 4         {
 5           test: /\.css$/,
 6           use: [
 7             'style-loader',
 8             'css-loader'
 9           ]
10         }
11       ]
12     }
13   };
```

The above configuration demonstrates the use of the `module` property, which is an object containing rules for different types of modules. Each rule is specified as an object in the `rules` array. The `test` property uses a regular expression to identify files based on their extensions—in this case, `.css` files. The `use` property then defines an array of loaders to be applied to these files, starting from the last to the first in the array.

For a more advanced setup, incorporating CSS preprocessors such as SASS, LESS, or Stylus is common. As an example, to integrate SASS processing, the `sass-loader` along with node-sass need to be installed and configured:

```
 1   module.exports = {
```

```
 2   module: {
 3     rules: [
 4       {
 5         test: /\.s[ac]ss$/,
 6         use: [
 7           'style-loader',
 8           'css-loader',
 9           'sass-loader'
10         ]
11       }
12     ]
13   }
14 };
```

In this configuration, the regular expression in the test property is updated to match both .sass and .scss file extensions. The sass-loader is then added to the use array, making sure it is placed after the css-loader but before the style-loader to maintain the correct order of processing.

To ensure Webpack processes CSS files correctly, the appropriate loader packages must be installed via npm or Yarn. This is done as follows:

```
 1   npm install --save-dev style-loader css-loader sass-loader node-sass
```

or, for Yarn users:

```
 1   yarn add --dev style-loader css-loader sass-loader node-sass
```

Upon execution of the above commands, the necessary loaders are added to the project's development dependencies, thereby enabling Webpack to process CSS and SASS files.

By configuring Webpack to understand and process CSS files along with their preprocessors, the development process becomes more streamlined, and developers can take advantage of CSS's full capabilities within a modular application architecture.

7.2   Incorporating CSS Loaders and Style Loaders

To effectively incorporate CSS into the Webpack build process, it is essential to understand the roles of `css-loader` and `style-loader`. These are modules that enable Webpack to process and bundle CSS files along with JavaScript files. The configuration of these loaders in the Webpack configuration file is a crucial step in ensuring that CSS integrates smoothly with the JavaScript module system.

The `css-loader` interprets `@import` and `url()` like import/require() and will resolve them. It takes a CSS file and returns the CSS with imports and URLs resolved via Webpack's require mechanism. In simple terms, it processes the CSS file, enabling the import of CSS files into JavaScript files, hence integrating styles directly within the Webpack build.

On the other hand, the `style-loader` injects the CSS into the DOM by appending a $<\$style\$>$ tag within the $<\$head\$>$ tag of the HTML document.   This loader is often used in development environments to enable hot reloading of CSS without reloading the entire page.   However, for production environments, it's recommended to use the `MiniCssExtractPlugin` to extract the CSS into separate files, which can be loaded asynchronously to reduce initial load times.

To configure both `css-loader` and `style-loader` in the Webpack configuration, include them in the module rules for CSS files as follows:

```
module.exports = {
    module: {
        rules: [
            {
                test: /\.css$/,
                use: ['style-loader', 'css-loader']
            }
        ]
    }
};
```

This configuration specifies that for every file ending in `.css`, Webpack should use the `css-loader` to process the CSS file and then use the `style-loader` to inject the CSS into the DOM. The use property is an array that specifies the loaders in the order they should be applied, meaning the `css-loader` processes the CSS file first, followed by the application of the `style-loader`.

For managing CSS in a production environment, it's crucial to extract the CSS into separate files. This can be achieved using the `MiniCssExtractPlugin`. Here is an example configuration that utilizes this plugin:

```
const MiniCssExtractPlugin = require('mini-css-extract-plugin');

module.exports = {
    module: {
        rules: [
            {
                test: /\.css$/,
                use: [MiniCssExtractPlugin.loader, 'css-loader']
            }
        ]
    },
    plugins: [
        new MiniCssExtractPlugin({
            filename: '[name].css',
            chunkFilename: '[id].css',
        }),
    ]
};
```

In this setup, the `MiniCssExtractPlugin.loader` replaces the `style-loader`, extracting CSS into separate, cacheable files rather than injecting them into the DOM. This approach is beneficial for improving page load performance and is typically recommended for production builds.

Incorporating CSS and style loaders into Webpack configuration allows developers to seamlessly integrate CSS into their JavaScript applications, providing a robust methodology for managing styles across development and production environments.

7.3   Utilizing Preprocessors: SASS, LESS, and Stylus

Utilizing CSS preprocessors such as SASS, LESS, and Stylus significantly enriches the capability of CSS by introducing features like variables, nested rules, and functions. These preprocessors allow for more maintainable and concise stylesheets by compiling extended stylesheet languages down to standard CSS. Integrating these preprocessors with Webpack involves configuring 'sass-loader', 'less-loader', and 'stylus-loader' respectively.

First, let's address the installation of these loaders. For each preprocessor, the corresponding loader and the preprocessor itself must be installed. For SASS, both 'sass-loader' and 'node-sass' are required. Similarly, 'less-loader' and 'less' for LESS, and 'stylus-loader' with 'stylus' for Stylus. This can be achieved using npm or yarn.

```
1  npm install --save-dev sass-loader node-sass
2  npm install --save-dev less-loader less
3  npm install --save-dev stylus-loader stylus
```

Once installed, the next step is to configure these loaders in the Webpack configuration file. This involves modifying the 'module.rules' array to include a rule for each preprocessor type. Each rule uses a regular expression to test for file extensions (.scss for SASS, .less for LESS, and .styl for Stylus) and specifies the loaders in a 'use' array.

```
1  module.exports = {
2    module: {
3      rules: [
4        {
5          test: /\.scss$/,
6          use: [
7            'style-loader',
8            'css-loader',
9            'sass-loader'
10         ]
11       },
12       {
13         test: /\.less$/,
14         use: [
15           'style-loader',
16           'css-loader',
17           'less-loader'
18         ]
```

```
19      },
20      {
21        test: /\.styl$/,
22        use: [
23          'style-loader',
24          'css-loader',
25          'stylus-loader'
26        ]
27      }
28    ]
29  }
30 };
```

When using these preprocessors, it's vital to understand their unique features and how they can benefit your development process. For instance, SASS offers a comprehensive feature set including mixins, inheritance, and more, making it ideal for complex projects. LESS, on the other hand, offers simpler syntax and JavaScript evaluation, which can be beneficial for smaller projects or those heavily utilizing JavaScript. Stylus provides a very flexible syntax that can be appealing for developers looking for brevity and expressiveness.

Additionally, to effectively integrate with Webpack, understanding the specific options each loader offers for customization is crucial. For 'sass-loader', options like 'sassOptions' provide a way to configure the underlying node-sass library.

```
1  {
2    test: /\.scss$/,
3    use: [
4      'style-loader',
5      'css-loader',
6      {
7        loader: 'sass-loader',
8        options: {
9          sassOptions: {
10            outputStyle: 'compressed',
11          },
12        },
13      },
14    ],
15  }
```

Applying preprocessors like SASS, LESS, and Stylus within a Webpack-configured environment helps to enhance CSS management and maintainability. Proper installation and configuration of the corresponding loaders are crucial steps towards utilizing these powerful tools. Additionally, leveraging the unique features and benefits of each preprocessor can significantly influence the efficiency and scalability of a project's styling architecture.

7.4 Setting Up PostCSS for Autoprefixing and Optimizations

Setting up PostCSS for autoprefixing and optimizations in a Webpack environment involves configuring PostCSS as a tool to process CSS with JavaScript. PostCSS offers a powerful ecosystem of plugins, including autoprefixer and cssnano, which are indispensable for ensuring cross-browser compatibility and optimizing the final CSS bundle size.

The initial step involves installing the necessary packages. For a standard Webpack configuration, this means including PostCSS, autoprefixer, cssnano, and postcss-loader. This can be done via the npm package manager.

```
1   npm install --save-dev postcss autoprefixer cssnano postcss-loader
```

Once the installation is complete, the next step is to configure PostCSS by creating a postcss.config.js file at the root of the project. This configuration file is essential for defining the plugins that PostCSS will use.

```
1   module.exports = {
2     plugins: [
3       require('autoprefixer'),
4       require('cssnano')({
5         preset: 'default',
6       }),
7     ],
8   };
```

In this configuration, the 'autoprefixer' plugin is responsible for adding browser-specific prefixes to CSS rules using values from Can I Use. It is invaluable for maintaining cross-browser compatibility without manually adding these prefixes. The 'cssnano' plugin is a CSS minifier that consolidates many small optimizations into one step, significantly reducing the CSS file size for production deployments.

With the postcss.config.js file in place, the next step is incorporating PostCSS into the Webpack configuration. This involves modifying the webpack.config.js file to include the postcss-loader in the module rules for CSS files.

```
module: {
  rules: [
    {
      test: /\.css$/,
      use: [
        'style-loader',
        'css-loader',
        'postcss-loader'
      ]
    }
  ]
}
```

By adding 'postcss-loader' after 'css-loader' and before 'style-loader' in the array, it ensures that PostCSS processes the CSS right after it is loaded and before it is injected into the DOM or extracted by other plugins.

One of the paramount benefits of this setup is the automation of vendor prefixing. Developers no longer need to worry about which CSS properties require prefixes for specific browsers. The autoprefixer plugin utilises the data from Can I Use to apply the necessary prefixes, ensuring that the CSS works across a broad spectrum of browsers.

The optimization step powered by 'cssnano' plays a crucial role in production builds. By compressing the CSS, removing comments, whitespaces, and merging rules where possible, 'cssnano' significantly reduces the size of the CSS, enhancing the performance of the web application.

For projects requiring more control over the CSS processing, further customization of PostCSS plugins can be done as needed. The PostCSS ecosystem offers a wide range of plugins for almost every conceivable CSS processing requirement, making it a versatile tool for both development and production environments.

In summary, setting up PostCSS with autoprefixing and optimization plugins in a Webpack project streamlines the development process, automatically handling cross-browser compatibility issues and optimizing CSS for production, thereby improving both the developer experience and the performance of the web application.

7.5   Isolating Component Styles with CSS Modules

Isolating component styles in a large-scale web application is essential for maintaining a scalable and manageable codebase. CSS Modules provide a straightforward and efficient method for achieving such isolation.   This approach localizes CSS by automatically generating unique class and animation names, thus preventing global scope pollution and style conflicts across components.

To begin integrating CSS Modules into a Webpack project, specific loaders are required.   The primary loaders for this task are `css-loader` and `style-loader`.   However, configuring the `css-loader` is vital for enabling CSS Modules. The configuration involves modifying the Webpack configuration file (`webpack.config.js`) as follows:

```
1   module.exports = {
2     module: {
3       rules: [
4         {
5           test: /\.css$/,
6           use: [
7             'style-loader',
8             {
9               loader: 'css-loader',
10              options: {
11                modules: true,
12                localIdentName: '[name]__[local]___[hash:base64:5]',
13              },
14            },
15          ],
16        },
```

```
17      ],
18    },
19  };
```

In this configuration, the test property identifies files ending with
.css as the target for this rule. The use property specifies an array
of loaders to apply. Importantly, the css-loader is configured with
modules: true to enable CSS Modules. The localIdentName
option allows customization of the generated class names, which is
a combination of the component name, the local name (class name
defined in the CSS file), and a hash for uniqueness.

With CSS Modules enabled, stylesheets are imported directly into
JavaScript component files, and styles are referenced as object
properties. Consider the following example:

```
1  import React from 'react';
2  import styles from './App.module.css';
3
4  function App() {
5    return <div className={styles.container}>Hello, world!</div>;
6  }
```

In this example, App.module.css is imported with a named import
styles. The CSS class .container defined in App.module.css is accessed as styles.container within the JavaScript file. This encapsu-
lation ensures that the .container class is localized to the App component, avoiding conflicts with other CSS classes named container
in the project.

```
.App__container___1a2b3c {
  background-color: #f0f0f0;
  padding: 20px;
}
```

The output class name .App__container___1a2b3c is a transformed
version of the original class name, ensuring uniqueness and preventing style leakage.

In summary, CSS Modules significantly streamline the process of
isolating component styles in a Webpack-configured environment.
By localizing styles, developers can avoid common issues related to
global CSS, such as unintended overrides and conflicts. Moreover,

the setup process is straightforward, involving modifications to the Webpack configuration and adopting a specific pattern for importing and using styles within components.

7.6   Integration of CSS Frameworks like Bootstrap and Tailwind

Integration of CSS frameworks such as Bootstrap and Tailwind into a Webpack-managed project significantly streamlines the development process by providing pre-designed components and utility classes that enhance both the efficiency and aesthetics of web applications.   This section will cover the steps required to incorporate these frameworks into your Webpack build.

Bootstrap Integration

To integrate Bootstrap, first, you need to install it alongside jQuery and Popper.js, which are Bootstrap's dependencies, using npm or yarn.

```
1   npm install bootstrap jquery popper.js --save
```

Next, you will need to configure Webpack to handle Bootstrap's CSS and JavaScript files. For CSS, ensure that style-loader and css-loader are configured in your webpack.config.js file, as previously discussed. To import Bootstrap's JavaScript component library, you might need to add ProvidePlugin to your Webpack configuration to automatically load jQuery and Popper.js wherever they're referenced.

```
1   const webpack = require('webpack');
2
3   module.exports = {
4     // Existing configuration
5     plugins: [
6       new webpack.ProvidePlugin({
7         $: 'jquery',
8         jQuery: 'jquery',
9         'window.jQuery': 'jquery',
```

```
10       Popper: ['popper.js', 'default']
11     })
12   ]
13 };
```

To utilize Bootstrap's CSS, simply import it in your entry JavaScript file.

```
1  import 'bootstrap/dist/css/bootstrap.min.css';
```

Tailwind CSS Integration

Tailwind CSS takes a utility-first approach to styling, in contrast to the component-based structure of Bootstrap. To integrate Tailwind CSS into your project, start by installing it and its peer-dependencies via npm or yarn.

```
1  npm install tailwindcss postcss autoprefixer --save-dev
```

The next step involves creating a Tailwind configuration file, which can be easily done through Tailwind's CLI utility.

```
1  npx tailwindcss init
```

This command generates a 'tailwind.config.js' file in your project root, allowing you to customize your design system.

You will also need a PostCSS configuration file to compile Tailwind. Create a 'postcss.config.js' file and configure it to use Tailwind and Autoprefixer.

```
1  module.exports = {
2    plugins: [
3      require('tailwindcss'),
4      require('autoprefixer'),
5    ]
6  };
```

Finally, include Tailwind in your CSS by importing it into your main CSS file.

```
1  @tailwind base;
2  @tailwind components;
3  @tailwind utilities;
```

189

Optimization Note: For both Bootstrap and Tailwind, consider employing CSS tree-shaking tools like PurgeCSS to remove unused styles, vastly decreasing the filesize of your final CSS bundle. Integration with PurgeCSS can be done through Webpack's configuration, improving the performance of your application.

Note: The precise implementation details for PurgeCSS will vary based on the version of Webpack and other build tools you are using. Consult the latest PurgeCSS documentation for the most up-to-date instructions.

Integrating CSS frameworks like Bootstrap and Tailwind into your Webpack setup enhances your web development workflow by providing a vast array of pre-designed components and utility classes. Each framework presents a different approach to styling web applications, and the choice between them should be influenced by the specific needs of your project and personal or team preferences. By following the outlined steps and ensuring proper configuration in your Webpack setup, you can effectively leverage these frameworks to create visually appealing and responsive web applications.

7.7   Using PurgeCSS for Removing Unused CSS

Let's delve into the utilization of PurgeCSS for the elimination of unnecessary CSS. This step is fundamental in enhancing the performance and loading speed of web applications by stripping away CSS rules that are not used in the project files.

PurgeCSS analyzes your content files, such as HTML, Pug, JavaScript, and any other templates or components where classes and ids might be referenced. It then matches these references against the CSS files in your project and removes the styles that are not found in your content.

To integrate PurgeCSS with a Webpack build process, several steps need to be followed. The primary approach involves installing PurgeCSS and configuring it within the Webpack configuration file.

First, PurgeCSS should be added to your project through npm or yarn:

```
1  npm install @fullhuman/postcss-purgecss --save-dev
```

or

```
1  yarn add @fullhuman/postcss-purgecss --dev
```

Once installed, the next step is to configure it within your Webpack setup. This typically involves modifying your 'postcss.config.js' file, assuming PostCSS is already being used in your project. If not, you'll need to first set up PostCSS with Webpack.

In the 'postcss.config.js' file, incorporate PurgeCSS as follows:

```
1  module.exports = {
2    plugins: [
3      require('@fullhuman/postcss-purgecss')({
4        content: ['./src/**/*.html', './src/**/*.vue', './src/**/*.jsx'],
5        defaultExtractor: content => content.match(/[\w-/:]+(?<!:)/g) || []
6      }),
7      require('autoprefixer'),
8    ],
9  }
```

This configuration specifies the paths to the content files that should be analyzed ('content' array) and defines a 'defaultExtractor' function. The 'defaultExtractor' function is crucial for accurately identifying the classes and ids utilized in your project, facilitating their comparison against the CSS files.

It is recommended to encapsulate this configuration with environment checks to ensure that PurgeCSS is only employed in the production build process, preserving all CSS rules in the development environment for debugging purposes.

```
1  if (process.env.NODE_ENV === 'production') {
2    module.exports.plugins.push(
3      require('@fullhuman/postcss-purgecss')({
4        // Configuration options
5      })
6    )
7  }
```

After configuring PurgeCSS properly, the Webpack build process will automatically remove all unused CSS when generating a production build. This results in significantly smaller CSS file sizes, leading to faster load times and an improved user experience.

It is crucial to test the production build thoroughly to ensure that no necessary styles have been inadvertently removed. In some cases, dynamically generated classes (for instance, from a JavaScript function) might not be detected by PurgeCSS. Specific strategies, such as explicitly including such classes in a whitelist or using patterns to match dynamically generated class names, can be employed to address these instances.

- Enhances performance by removing unused CSS.

- Must be carefully configured to avoid missing styles.

- Should be incorporated into the production build process.

- Requires thorough testing to ensure necessary styles are preserved.

PurgeCSS can significantly contribute to optimizing your Webpack build by minimizing the size of the CSS bundle, but it demands meticulous configuration and testing to strike a balance between performance gains and styling integrity.

7.8 Optimizing   CSS   Delivery   for Performance

Optimizing the delivery of CSS is crucial in enhancing the performance of web applications. Performance optimizations specifically aimed at CSS delivery are targeted to reduce render-blocking resources, decrease load times, and improve the overall user experience. This section will explore various strategies to optimize CSS delivery, including critical path CSS implementation, non-blocking loading techniques, and the use of the MiniCssExtractPlugin.

One effective approach to optimize CSS delivery is the extraction of critical path CSS. Critical path CSS refers to the minimal set of styles necessary to render the visible portion of the web page. By identifying and inlining these styles directly into the HTML document, we can significantly reduce render-blocking time. This practice ensures that the content above the fold is styled and rendered as quickly as possible, thereby improving perceived performance.

```
const Critters = require('critters-webpack-plugin');

module.exports = {
  plugins: [
    new Critters({
      // Options for extracting & inlining critical path CSS
      preload: 'swap',
      pruneSource: false,
      reduceInlineStyles: false,
      inlineFonts: true,
    })
  ]
};
```

The above Webpack configuration snippet demonstrates how to integrate the Critters plugin, a useful tool for handling critical path CSS. It provides several options to fine-tune how critical styles are extracted, preloaded, and inlined.

Another method to optimize CSS delivery is to enable non-blocking loading of non-critical CSS. This can be achieved by loading the remaining stylesheets asynchronously using JavaScript or by employing the rel="preload" attribute in combination with as="style" on link elements.

```
<link rel="preload" href="styles.css" as="style" onload="this.onload=null;this.
    rel='stylesheet'">
<noscript><link rel="stylesheet" href="styles.css"></noscript>
```

This markup preloads the stylesheet asynchronously and applies it once loaded, ensuring that it does not block the rendering of the page. The noscript tag provides a fallback for scenarios where JavaScript is disabled.

Finally, the MiniCssExtractPlugin is pivotal for optimizing CSS delivery. It extracts CSS into separate files, one for each JavaScript entry point. These standalone CSS files are then loaded asynchronously or paralleled, providing an additional performance boost by leveraging browser caching more efficiently and reducing the initial payload.

```
1   const MiniCssExtractPlugin = require('mini-css-extract-plugin');
2
3   module.exports = {
4     module: {
5       rules: [
6         {
7           test: /\.css$/,
8           use: [MiniCssExtractPlugin.loader, 'css-loader']
9         }
10      ]
11    },
12    plugins: [
13      new MiniCssExtractPlugin({
14        // Options: specifying the output file name pattern
15        filename: '[name].[contenthash].css',
16      })
17    ]
18  };
```

This configuration extracts CSS from your JavaScript bundles, generating a separate CSS file for each bundle. By specifying a content hash in the filename, it ensures that each file is cache-busted when its content changes, an important practice for long-term caching strategies.

Optimizing CSS delivery involves a combination of critical CSS extraction, non-blocking loading techniques, and leveraging plugins like MiniCssExtractPlugin for better payload and caching management. Each of these strategies contributes to a faster, more performant web application, enhancing both the actual and perceived performance for the end-user.

7.9   Source Maps for CSS Debugging

Debugging CSS within modern web development workflows can pose significant challenges, especially when using pre-processors such as SASS, LESS, or Stylus. The code written by developers undergoes multiple transformations before reaching the browser, complicating the direct correlation between the source code and the final rendered result. This disconnect can hinder efficient debugging and development. Source maps play a pivotal role in alleviating these challenges by providing a bridge between the original source code and the transformed code delivered to the browser.

Source maps contain information that maps the transformed source to the original source, allowing developers to debug their original CSS or pre-processed code directly in the browser's developer tools. This capability not only enhances the debugging process but also significantly speeds up development and troubleshooting. Webpack, as a module bundler, offers built-in support for generating source maps through a simple configuration adjustment.

To enable CSS source maps in Webpack, one must configure both the style-related loaders and the development tool settings within the Webpack configuration file. Below is an illustration of how to adjust the Webpack configuration to include source maps for CSS debugging:

```
module.exports = {
  devtool: 'source-map', // Enable source map support
  module: {
    rules: [
      {
        test: /\.css$/, // Target CSS files
        use: [
          'style-loader', // Inject CSS into the DOM
          {
            loader: 'css-loader', // The css-loader interprets @import and url()
              like import/require() and will resolve them.
            options: {
              sourceMap: true, // Enable source map generation for css-loader
            },
          },
        ],
      },
      {
        test: /\.s[ac]ss$/, // Target SASS/SCSS files
        use: [
          'style-loader', // Injects styles into the DOM
          {
            loader: 'css-loader',
            options: {
              sourceMap: true, // Enable source map generation
            },
          },
          {
            loader: 'sass-loader', // Compiles Sass to CSS
            options: {
              sourceMap: true, // Enable source map generation for sass-loader
            },
```

```
32          },
33        ],
34          },
35      ],
36    },
37  };
```

With the above configuration, Webpack generates source maps for CSS. These maps correlate the styles seen in the browser's developer tools directly back to the individual source files, even if those styles were originally written in a pre-processed language like SASS.

Upon inspecting an element within the browser's developer tools, instead of showing the compiled CSS line number, it will display the original source file name and line number, significantly improving the efficiency of pinpointing and rectifying issues.

Moreover, enabling source maps does not noticeably impact the build process during development. However, it is advisable to disable or modify the source map generation for production builds to secure source code and improve load times. This guidance is achieved by adjusting the `devtool` configuration in the Webpack configuration file accordingly for production environments.

Integrating source maps into the development workflow bridges the gap between the high-level, abstracted code written by developers and the final rendered output. This integration empowers developers to retain the advantages of CSS pre-processing and modular development, without sacrificing the efficiency and effectiveness of debugging processes.

7.10   Implementing Critical Path CSS for Faster Rendering

Critical Path CSS involves identifying and inlining the minimal amount of CSS necessary to render the visible portion of your web page, also known as "above the fold" content. This technique significantly reduces the time to first render of your webpage, providing an enhanced user experience, particularly for those on slower network connections or devices. Below, we explore the methodology for creating and incorporating Critical Path CSS in a Webpack project.

Identifying Critical CSS

The first step in implementing Critical Path CSS is to identify what styles are actually critical to your page's initial render. While automated tools exist to assist in this process, understanding the basic criteria for what makes CSS critical can be beneficial:

- Styles that format the layout and structure of the "above the fold" content.

- Essential font styles, colors, and visibility properties.

- Immediate interactive elements such as buttons or input fields visible to the user at the initial load.

Generating Critical CSS

Various tools and packages are available to help automate the extraction of Critical Path CSS, such as PurgeCSS, Critical, and web-based services like Penthouse. When using these tools within a Webpack configuration, the process typically involves the following steps:

```
1   const CriticalPlugin = require('webpack-plugin-critical').CriticalPlugin;
2
3   module.exports = {
4       plugins: [
5           new CriticalPlugin({
6               base: 'dist/',
7               src: 'index.html',
8               inline: true,
9               minify: true,
10              extract: true,
11              width: 1300,
12              height: 900,
13              penthouse: {
14                  blockJSRequests: false,
15              }
16          })
```

```
17      ]
18    };
```

In the example above, the `CriticalPlugin` is configured to extract, minify, and inline the Critical Path CSS from the `'index.html'` file located in the `'dist/'` directory. The specified `width` and `height` dimensions emulate a typical viewport for "above the fold" content.

Inlining Critical CSS in HTML

After generating the Critical Path CSS, the next step is to inline these styles directly into the `<head>` of your HTML document. This is crucial for achieving faster perceived loading times since the browser does not have to wait for external stylesheets to download and parse before rendering the page.

The `CriticalPlugin` illustrated previously automatically inlines the generated Critical Path CSS. If opting for a different approach or tool, ensure the process entails embedding the Critical CSS within a `<style>` tag in the document's `<head>`, as shown below:

```
<head>
    <style>
        /* Critical Path CSS */
    </style>
</head>
```

Deferring Non-Critical CSS

To prevent render-blocking, non-critical external CSS files should be loaded asynchronously or deferred until after the initial page render. This can be achieved by using the `preload` attribute with a `<link>` tag, followed by JavaScript to change the `rel` attribute to `stylesheet` once the page has loaded:

```
1    <link rel="preload" href="main.css" as="style" onload="this.rel='stylesheet'">
2    <noscript><link rel="stylesheet" href="main.css"></noscript>
```

The `<noscript>` tag ensures that users with JavaScript disabled still receive the full-styled site, albeit with a potentially longer load time.

Implementing Critical Path CSS requires diligence and an understanding of your user's needs and behaviors. While the setup process might seem intricate at first, the performance gains and user experience improvements make the effort worthwhile. Coupling Webpack with the right plugins and techniques streamlines generating, inlining, and deferring CSS, ensuring your web application is fast, responsive, and engaging from the first pixel rendered.

7.11   Managing Global and Local Styles in Single Page Applications

In single-page applications (SPAs), style management involves a strategic approach to distinguish between global styles that affect the entire application and local styles specific to individual components. This distinction is crucial for maintaining a consistent look and feel while ensuring that component-specific styles do not leak into the global namespace, potentially causing unintended side effects.

Global styles typically include base styles, such as resets or normalizations, typography, grid systems, and utility classes. These are applied universally and provide a cohesive appearance throughout the application. In contrast, local styles are applied to individual components and define their specific appearance without influencing other parts of the application.

To manage global and local styles effectively in the context of Webpack, several techniques and configurations are employed. The first step involves setting up the appropriate loaders within the Webpack configuration file.

```
1  module.exports = {
2    module: {
3      rules: [
4        {
5          test: /\.css$/,
6          use: ['style-loader', 'css-loader']
7        }
8      ]
```

199

```
 9      }
10    };
```

The configuration above enables Webpack to process CSS files using the `css-loader` and inject them into the DOM using the `style-loader`. However, to differentiate between global and local styles, additional configurations and conventions are needed.

CSS Modules offer a straightforward solution for isolating local styles. By enabling CSS Modules in Webpack's `css-loader` options, class names and animation names are scoped locally by default. This can be configured as follows:

```
1    {
2      loader: 'css-loader',
3      options: {
4        modules: true
5      }
6    }
```

With CSS Modules, local styles are kept local to the component, and class names are automatically generated in a way that minimizes the risk of conflict with global styles.

For global styles, it's common practice to create a separate CSS entry point in the Webpack configuration and explicitly import global style sheets. This ensures that global styles are loaded and applied universally, while component-specific styles are managed through CSS Modules.

Webpack also facilitates the organization of CSS into separate chunks, ensuring that styles are loaded as needed, rather than in a monolithic bundle. This is particularly beneficial for SPAs, where not all components are loaded immediately.

```
 1    module.exports = {
 2      optimization: {
 3        splitChunks: {
 4          cacheGroups: {
 5            styles: {
 6              name: 'styles',
 7              test: /\.css$/,
 8              chunks: 'all',
 9              enforce: true
10            }
11          }
```

```
12      }
13    }
14  };
```

In the context of SPAs, managing global and local styles requires careful consideration of how styles are bundled and applied. By utilizing mechanisms such as CSS Modules and strategically configuring Webpack, developers can achieve an effective separation of global and local styles, enhancing both the scalability and maintainability of their applications.

7.12 Optimizing CSS Assets with MiniCssExtractPlugin

Optimizing CSS assets is a pivotal step in fine-tuning the performance of web applications. The MiniCssExtractPlugin is a plugin for Webpack that extracts CSS from your bundles into separate files. This process is critical for producing non-JavaScript assets (like CSS) that can be loaded in parallel, improving the loading time of web applications significantly.

Firstly, to utilize the MiniCssExtractPlugin, it must be installed and included in your Webpack configuration. This can be done by running the npm command to install the plugin:

```
1  npm install --save-dev mini-css-extract-plugin
```

After installation, you include it in your Webpack configuration file by requiring it at the top of the file and then adding it to the plugins array:

```
1  const MiniCssExtractPlugin = require('mini-css-extract-plugin');
2
3  module.exports = {
4    // Other configuration options...
5    plugins: [new MiniCssExtractPlugin({
6      filename: '[name].[contenthash].css',
7      chunkFilename: '[id].[contenthash].css',
8    })],
9  };
```

The configuration above specifies the output file names for the extracted CSS. The `filename` option is used for the name of the CSS file(s) generated from the entry chunks, and `chunkFilename` is used for CSS files generated from the child chunks (Commonly used for lazy-loaded chunks). Utilizing `contenthash` in the file names enables cache busting by ensuring file names are updated when the content changes.

Beyond simply extracting CSS, optimization is crucial. The `MiniCssExtractPlugin` can be combined with `OptimizeCSSAssetsPlugin` to compress the extracted CSS files, reducing their size for faster network transfers.

To implement CSS compression, install the `OptimizeCSSAssetsPlugin`:

```
1  npm install --save-dev optimize-css-assets-webpack-plugin
```

Then, integrate it into the Webpack configuration as follows:

```
1   const OptimizeCSSAssetsPlugin = require('optimize-css-assets-webpack-plugin');
2
3   module.exports = {
4     optimization: {
5       minimizer: [
6         new OptimizeCSSAssetsPlugin({}),
7       ],
8     },
9     // Other configuration options...
10  };
```

This setup directs Webpack to use `OptimizeCSSAssetsPlugin` for CSS optimization tasks, such as minification. The empty object passed to `OptimizeCSSAssetsPlugin` can be replaced with options to further customize the behavior of the CSS optimization process.

In summary, the `MiniCssExtractPlugin` enables the extraction of CSS into separate files, which can significantly enhance the loading efficiency of a web application. Coupled with optimization techniques, such as compression using `OptimizeCSSAssetsPlugin`, it ensures the delivery of minimal, efficient CSS to the client, contributing to faster page rendering and an improved user experience.

Chapter 8

Managing Assets and Images

Efficient management of assets and images is essential for optimizing web applications, and this chapter provides a comprehensive guide to handling these resources within a Webpack environment. It explores the configuration and use of loaders such as file-loader and url-loader for managing image files, fonts, and other static resources. Additionally, the chapter offers insight into advanced techniques for image optimization, including compression, lazy loading of images, and responsive images setup using srcset. By applying the practices outlined in this chapter, developers will be able to effectively organize and optimize assets and images, leading to faster load times and a more responsive user experience.

8.1   Overview of Asset Management in Webpack

Asset management is a fundamental aspect of web development, encompassing the organization and processing of external files such as images, fonts, stylesheets, and JavaScript files. Webpack, a powerful module bundler, streamlines this process through an extensive ecosystem of loaders and plugins, automating the transformation and optimization of assets. This section elucidates the core concepts of asset management within a Webpack environment.

Webpack treats every file as a module. This includes not just JavaScript files, but also CSS, images, fonts, and more. By leveraging Webpack's capabilities, developers can incorporate various types of assets into their build process, enhancing the performance and efficiency of web applications. The primary mechanism for handling these assets in Webpack is through the use of loaders and plugins.

- Loaders: Loaders in Webpack transform the files before they are added to the bundle. For example, the `file-loader` handles files such as images and fonts by copying them to the output directory and renaming them to avoid naming collisions. Similarly, the `url-loader` can transform files into base64 URIs, embedding them directly into the bundle to reduce the number of server requests.

- Plugins: Plugins are more potent tools in Webpack that can perform a wider range of tasks. They can be used to optimize the bundle, manage assets more effectively, and even define environment variables. The `ImageMinimizerPlugin`, for instance, optimizes images by compressing them without losing quality, thereby improving the load time of web applications.

Configuration of these loaders and plugins is done within the `webpack.config.js` file. A unique aspect of Webpack's asset management is its ability to understand dependencies. Webpack analyzes the asset requirements of every module and ensures that no asset is loaded before it is needed. This results in optimized loading, which is crucial for performance.

To integrate loaders into a Webpack configuration, the `module` field is used, specifying rules for different file types. For instance, to use the `file-loader` for image and font files, the following configuration might be employed:

```
1   module: {
2       rules: [
3           {
4               test: /\.(png|svg|jpg|gif|woff|woff2|eot|ttf|otf)$/,
5               use: [
6                   'file-loader'
7               ]
8           }
9       ]
10  }
```

This configuration directs Webpack to use the `file-loader` for files matching the regular expression. Each type of file (e.g., .png, .svg, etc.) is processed by the loader, consolidating them into the output directory as part of the build process.

Additionally, asset modules introduced in Webpack 5 offer a streamlined way of handling assets without configuring additional loaders. This feature simplifies the configuration, providing default loaders for various asset types. For example, the `type: 'asset/resource'` option replicates the functionality of the `file-loader`, automatically relocating files and generating unique filenames.

Mastering asset management in Webpack requires understanding its versatile ecosystem of loaders and plugins. By configuring Webpack to efficiently process various types of files, developers can significantly enhance the performance and responsiveness of web applications. The subsequent sections delve into specific strategies and configurations for optimizing asset handling in greater detail.

8.2   Configuring   Webpack   for   Image Optimization

Configuring Webpack for effective image optimization involves understanding and implementing specific loaders and plugins that reduce the size of images, thereby enhancing the performance of a web application.   This configuration aids in striking a balance between maintaining visual quality and ensuring fast load times, which is paramount for user experience and SEO rankings.

One of the initial steps in this process is the installation of necessary loaders and plugins. The image-minimizer-webpack-plugin and file-loader are pivotal in this setup. For installation, the following command lines are used:

```
npm install image-minimizer-webpack-plugin --save-dev
npm install file-loader --save-dev
```

After installing these tools, the next step is to configure them within the Webpack configuration file. The webpack.config.js file needs to be modified to include these loaders and plugins.

For the file-loader, it's utilized for processing image files and placing them into the output directory. To do this, you incorporate it into the module rules as shown below:

```
 1  module: {
 2    rules: [
 3      {
 4        test: /\.(png|svg|jpg|jpeg|gif)$/i,
 5        use: [
 6          {
 7            loader: 'file-loader',
 8            options: {
 9              outputPath: 'images',
10            },
11          },
12        ],
13      },
14    ],
15  }
```

This configuration ensures that image files encountered by Webpack during bundling are handled by the file-loader, which then outputs them into a specified directory, often named 'images'.

Following the `file-loader` configuration, the `image-minimizer-webpack-plugin` is introduced for image optimization. This plugin employs various compression techniques to reduce image file sizes without significant loss in quality. The plugin can be included in the Webpack configuration via the plugins array:

```
const ImageMinimizerPlugin = require('image-minimizer-webpack-plugin');

plugins: [
  new ImageMinimizerPlugin({
    minimizerOptions: {
      plugins: [
        ['gifsicle', { interlaced: true }],
        ['jpegtran', { progressive: true }],
        ['optipng', { optimizationLevel: 5 }],
        ['svgo', { plugins: [{ removeViewBox: false }] }],
      ],
    },
  }),
],
```

In the above configuration, `ImageMinimizerPlugin` is configured with several compression algorithms for different image formats like GIF, JPEG, PNG, and SVG. Each of these is tailored with specific options to ensure the best compromise between size and quality.

Additionally, Webpack offers an image optimization capability out-of-the-box with Asset Modules, which can serve as an alternative or complement to the `file-loader`:

```
module: {
  rules: [
    {
      test: /\.(png|svg|jpg|jpeg|gif)$/i,
      type: 'asset',
      parser: {
        dataUrlCondition: {
          maxSize: 8192,
        },
      },
    },
  ],
}
```

Asset Modules enable a more granular control over images, allowing smaller images to be inlined as Base64 strings, thereby reducing the number of HTTP requests, and larger images to be processed and emitted as separate files.

Employing these configurations within a Webpack setup considerably boosts performance by optimizing images, an essential asset type in web development. It's crucial to fine-tune these settings based on specific project needs to achieve the optimal balance between load times and image quality.

8.3   Using File Loader for Image and Font Assets

Managing static assets such as images and fonts effectively is crucial for optimizing web application performance. The `file-loader` in Webpack plays a significant role in handling these assets. It instructs Webpack on how to process these files and incorporate them into the output bundle, ultimately improving load times and enhancing the user experience.

To begin utilizing `file-loader`, it must first be installed. This can be achieved by running a command in the terminal:

```
1   npm install --save-dev file-loader
```

After installation, the next step involves configuring Webpack to use `file-loader` for managing image and font files. This is done by adding a rule to the module rules array in the Webpack configuration file (`webpack.config.js`).

```
1   module.exports = {
2     // Other configurations ...
3     module: {
4       rules: [
5         {
6           test: /\.(png|jpe?g|gif|svg)$/i,
7           use: [
8             {
9               loader: 'file-loader',
10              options: {
11                name: '[name].[ext]',
12                outputPath: 'images/',
13              },
14            },
```

```
15          ],
16        },
17        {
18          test: /\.(woff|woff2|eot|ttf|otf)$/i,
19          use: [
20            {
21              loader: 'file-loader',
22              options: {
23                name: '[name].[ext]',
24                outputPath: 'fonts/',
25              },
26            },
27          ],
28        },
29      ],
30    },
31    // Other configurations ...
32  };
```

In this configuration, two rules are defined for `file-loader`. The first rule targets image file formats (`.png`, `.jpeg`/`.jpg`, `.gif`, `.svg`) while the second rule is aimed at font formats (`.woff`, `.woff2`, `.eot`, `.ttf`, `.otf`).

Each rule includes a `test` property which utilizes a regular expression to match the file types, and a `use` property that specifies `file-loader` as the loader to be used. The `options` object within `file-loader` allows further customization. The `name` option defines the naming convention for the output files, and the `outputPath` option specifies the directory within the output bundle where these files will be placed.

By incorporating `file-loader` into your Webpack configuration, image and font assets are processed and bundled efficiently, ensuring they are properly loaded when your web application is accessed. This improves application load times and user experience by reducing request overheads and optimizing asset delivery.

For example, when a browser requests an HTML file containing an image tag referencing an asset managed by `file-loader`, Webpack ensures that the correct asset is served based on the configuration. The output path and file name adjustments made during the build process are respected, ensuring that the browser is served the correct, optimized asset.

To verify the configuration's effectiveness, you can run Webpack and observe the output:

```
1  npm run build
```

The console output should indicate that the specified image and font assets have been processed and output to the configured directories within the Webpack output directory. This is a clear indication that `file-loader` is properly set up and operational within your Webpack configuration.

`file-loader` serves as a vital tool in the management of static assets in Webpack-based projects. Proper configuration and integration of this loader into your project's build process ensure that images and fonts are efficiently handled, thereby optimizing overall application performance and user experience.

8.4 Leveraging URL Loader for Inline Images and Fonts

The URL Loader plays a pivotal role in the Webpack ecosystem by converting files into base64 URIs, thereby enabling the inline integration of assets such as images and fonts directly into your bundles. This capability significantly reduces the number of HTTP requests a browser must make, contributing to enhanced page load speeds and overall application performance.

To utilize the URL Loader for embedding images and fonts, it's necessary to first install the loader through npm or yarn. The installation command is as follows:

```
1  npm install url-loader --save-dev
```

or

```
1  yarn add url-loader --dev
```

Once installed, the URL Loader can be configured within the webpack.config.js file. Configuration entails specifying the module rules for handling specific file types. Below is an illustrative configuration snippet that demonstrates how to set up URL Loader for images:

```
module: {
  rules: [
    {
      test: /\.(png|svg|jpg|gif)$/,
      use: [
        {
          loader: 'url-loader',
          options: {
            limit: 8192,
            name: 'images/[name].[hash:7].[ext]',
          },
        },
      ],
    },
  ],
}
```

In the provided configuration, the test property utilizes a regular expression to match file names ending with png, svg, jpg, or gif extensions. The rules array specifies the use of URL Loader for these file types. The options object within the loader configuration includes two critical properties:

- The limit property, expressed in bytes, determines the maximum size of a file that can be inlined. Files exceeding this limit are not inlined but are instead subject to file-loader processing if file-loader is configured or output to the file system according to Webpack's file emission rules.

- The name property specifies the naming convention and directory structure for emitted files, applicable to files that are not inlined due to their size.

An analogous approach is used for fonts; however, the test condition in the webpack.config.js file's module rules section should be adjusted to match font file extensions, such as woff, woff2, ttf, eot, etc. For instance:

```
{
  test: /\.(woff|woff2|eot|ttf|otf)$/,
  use: [
    {
      loader: 'url-loader',
      options: {
        limit: 8192,
```

```
8          name: 'fonts/[name].[hash:7].[ext]',
9        },
10     },
11   ],
12 }
```

Incorporating URL Loader as demonstrated aids in enhancing the client-side performance of web applications by streamlining asset loading processes. It's crucial to tailor the limit parameter within the URL Loader's options to balance between the benefits of inlining small resource files and the potential performance drawbacks of excessively increasing the JavaScript bundle size. Experimentation and performance testing within the context of your specific application will guide the optimization of this parameter.

8.5   SVG Management: Inline SVG vs SVG Files

Managing Scalable Vector Graphics (SVG) efficiently is crucial for developers aiming to enhance the visual quality of web applications while keeping the performance overhead to a minimum. This section discusses two prevalent methods of SVG usage in Webpack environments: inline SVGs and SVG files. Each approach offers distinct advantages and considerations for implementation.

Inline SVGs refer to SVG code that is directly embedded within HTML documents. This method enables the immediate rendering of SVG content without the need for additional HTTP requests, thus potentially improving load times. Moreover, inline SVGs offer the advantage of being styled and manipulated via CSS and JavaScript directly in the HTML context. To include an SVG inline in a Webpack project, the svg-inline-loader can be utilized. Below is an example configuration for webpack.config.js to implement svg-inline-loader:

```
1 module.exports = {
2    module: {
3       rules: [
4          {
```

```
5        test: /\.svg$/,
6        use: ['svg-inline-loader'],
7      },
8    ],
9  },
10 };
```

The above configuration will preprocess all .svg files through svg-inline-loader, making them ready for inline inclusion in your components or HTML files.

SVG Files, on the other hand, are treated as external resources. This approach involves linking to SVG files as one would with images or other external assets. When SVGs are managed as separate files, browsers handle them with standard HTTP requests. This method is particularly beneficial when the same SVG content is reused across multiple pages, as it allows browsers to cache the SVG file efficiently, reducing the amount of data transferred over the network on subsequent page loads. To manage SVG files in Webpack, one can use the file-loader. The following snippet shows how to configure file-loader for SVG files within webpack.config.js:

```
1  module.exports = {
2    module: {
3      rules: [
4        {
5          test: /\.(svg)$/,
6          use: [
7            {
8              loader: 'file-loader',
9              options: {
10               name: '[name].[ext]',
11               outputPath: 'images/',
12             },
13           },
14         ],
15       },
16     ],
17   },
18 };
```

The configuration directs Webpack to process all .svg files with

213

`file-loader`, storing the output in a designated `images/` directory. This approach ensures that all SVG assets are efficiently managed and ready for web deployment.

Both inline and external SVG management strategies offer specific advantages. Inline SVGs provide superior performance for small, frequently used graphics and allow for more extensive manipulation via CSS and JavaScript. Meanwhile, SVG files are advantageous for caching purposes and when dealing with larger, less frequently used graphics. Selecting the appropriate method depends on the specific needs of the project and the performance considerations at play.

Best Practices for SVG management in Webpack environments include:

- Utilizing inline SVGs for small, reusable graphics that benefit from CSS and JS manipulation.

- Employing SVG files for larger graphics and icons that are used across multiple pages, taking advantage of browser caching.

- Leveraging Webpack loaders such as `svg-inline-loader` and `file-loader` to streamline the management process.

- Optimizing SVG assets for performance using tools like SVGO before incorporating them into a Webpack project.

Effectively managing SVGs within a Webpack setup enhances the performance and visual fidelity of web applications. Developers should carefully consider the trade-offs between inline SVGs and SVG files to determine the best approach for their specific use case.

8.6   Setting Up ImageMinimizerPlugin for Image Compression

Image optimization forms a corner-stone in enhancing web application performance. Among various optimization strategies, compression plays a pivotal role by reducing the file size of images, thereby speeding up load times significantly without compromising on quality. The ImageMinimizerPlugin is a popular choice within the Webpack ecosystem for accomplishing this task effectively.

Installation

First and foremost, it is prerequisite to have Webpack installed and configured in your project. Assuming that foundation is set, to begin utilizing ImageMinimizerPlugin, it needs to be installed. This can be done with the following npm command:

```
1  npm install image-minimizer-webpack-plugin imagemin imagemin-mozjpeg imagemin-
     pngquant --save-dev
```

This command installs the plugin along with imagemin and plugins for optimizing JPEG and PNG images specifically, namely imagemin-mozjpeg and imagemin-pngquant.

Configuration

Once installed, the next step involves integrating ImageMinimizerPlugin into your Webpack configuration. Update your Webpack configuration file, typically webpack.config.js, to include the plugin. This will involve importing the plugin at the top of your configuration file and adding a new section within the 'plugins' array.

```
1  const ImageMinimizerPlugin = require("image-minimizer-webpack-plugin");
2
3  module.exports = {
4    // Existing configuration options
5    plugins: [
6      // Other plugins
7      new ImageMinimizerPlugin({
8        minimizerOptions: {
9          plugins: [
10           ["imagemin-mozjpeg", { quality: 75 }],
11           ["imagemin-pngquant", { quality: [0.6, 0.8] }]
12         ],
13       },
14     }),
15   ],
16 };
```

In this configuration snippet, the plugin is setup with options for
JPEG and PNG compression. The 'quality' option for JPEG images
is set to 75, representing the compression quality. For PNG images,
the 'quality' is an array with two values signifying the range of
quality to aim for during compression.

Advanced Configuration: Optimization on Demand

A more advanced setup might involve compressing images only during the production build and not during development. This ensures
faster build times during development. Below is an example configuration demonstrating this technique:

```
1   const ImageMinimizerPlugin = require("image-minimizer-webpack-plugin");
2
3   module.exports = (env, argv) => {
4     const isProduction = argv.mode === 'production';
5
6     return {
7       // Other configuration options
8       plugins: [
9         // Other plugins
10        ...(isProduction ? [new ImageMinimizerPlugin({
11          minimizerOptions: {
12            plugins: [
13              ["imagemin-mozjpeg", { quality: 75 }],
14              ["imagemin-pngquant", { quality: [0.6, 0.8] }]
15            ],
16          },
17        })] : []),
18      ],
19    };
20  };
```

This configuration utilizes a function to export the Webpack configuration. It checks if the build mode is set to 'production'. If so, it
includes the ImageMinimizerPlugin in the plugins array; otherwise,
it omits it, skipping image compression during development.

Incorporating ImageMinimizerPlugin provides a robust solution
for image compression within a Webpack build process.   By
following   the   steps   outlined   above   for   installation   and
configuration, developers can achieve significant improvements in
their web application's load time and performance. Crucially, the
plugin   offers   flexibility   through   its   supportive   optimization

strategies, ensuring that quality is not sacrificed for efficiency.

8.7 Handling Videos and Other Media Types

With the growing demand for multimedia content in web applications, efficient management of videos and other media types has become crucial. This section will address how Webpack can be configured to handle such resources, ensuring they are optimized for a seamless user experience.

To manage videos and other non-image media files within a Webpack project, it is necessary to utilize appropriate loaders and plugins. The file-loader and url-loader are versatile tools that can also be applied to video files, similar to how they are used for images and fonts.

Using File Loader for Videos

The file-loader resolves the import/require() on a file into a url and emits the file into the output directory. To use file-loader for handling video files, include the following configuration in your webpack.config.js:

```
module.exports = {
  module: {
    rules: [
      {
        test: /\.(mp4|webm|ogg|mp3|wav|flac|aac)(\?.*)?$/,
        loader: 'file-loader',
        options: {
          name: 'media/[name].[hash:8].[ext]',
        },
      },
    ],
  },
};
```

This configuration will process files with extensions .mp4, .webm, .ogg, .mp3, .wav, .flac, and .aac, emitting them into the media/

folder within the output directory. The file name will be preserved, appended with an 8-character hash for cache busting, ensuring that updated files are reloaded by browsers.

Optimizing Video Files

While `file-loader` handles the inclusion and bundling of video files, it does not, by default, optimize them. Large video files can significantly impact load times and overall performance. To tackle this issue, employing a video compression tool during the pre-build phase is recommended.

One effective CLI tool for this purpose is FFmpeg. The following script demonstrates how FFmpeg can be used to compress a video file:

```
1   ffmpeg -i input.mp4 -vcodec h264 -acodec aac -strict -2 output.mp4
```

Run this script as part of your build process, or manually on your media files before including them in your project, to ensure that the videos are optimized for web delivery.

Integrating Responsive Videos

Just as with images, ensuring videos are responsive is key to maintaining a high-quality user experience across devices. HTML5 provides the `<video>` element, which can be made responsive through CSS styles. However, serving different video qualities based on the user's device and connection speed can enhance the experience further.

Here is an example of how to serve different video qualities using the `<source>` elements:

```
1   <video controls>
2     <source src="video_hd.mp4" type="video/mp4" media="screen and (min-width: 720px
        )">
3     <source src="video_sd.mp4" type="video/mp4">
4     Your browser does not support the video tag.
5   </video>
```

This `<video>` element includes two `<source>` elements, specifying high-definition and standard-definition versions of the video. The browser will select the appropriate source based on the device's screen width.

In summary, handling videos and other media types efficiently within a Webpack environment involves the appropriate use of loaders for bundling, optimizing media files for web delivery, and ensuring content is responsive. By leveraging Webpack configurations, compression tools, and responsive design techniques, developers can ensure their multimedia content is both performant and accessible.

8.8 Integrating Responsive Images with srcset

In the context of modern web development, ensuring images are both responsive and efficiently loaded is paramount. This section will discuss the implementation of responsive images using the srcset attribute in conjunction with Webpack configurations.

Responsive images are essentially about serving different image files to users based on the resolution and size of their viewing device. This not only improves the user experience by ensuring images are displayed appropriately across devices but also optimizes the load time by not downloading unnecessarily large files for smaller screens. The srcset attribute in HTML plays a crucial role in this solution.

First, let's cover how to configure Webpack to handle the image files that will be used with srcset. Webpack's asset modules, specifically the image assets, need to be configured to output the different sizes required.

```
1  module.exports = {
2    module: {
3      rules: [
4        {
5          test: /\.(png|jpe?g|gif)$/i,
6          type: 'asset/resource',
```

```
7      generator: {
8        filename: 'images/[name]-[width].[ext]',
9      },
10    },
11   ],
12  },
13 };
```

The above Webpack configuration includes a rule for image files (PNG, JPG/JPEG, GIF) that outputs them as resources. The key addition here is the generator configuration which customizes the output filename to include the image width, enabling the generation of multiple sized images from a single source image, necessary for responsive image setups.

Following the Webpack configuration, the next step involves actually writing the HTML code to utilize the srcset attribute for an image.

```
1 <img src="path/to/default-image.jpg"
2     srcset="path/to/image-480w.jpg 480w,
3             path/to/image-768w.jpg 768w,
4             path/to/image-1024w.jpg 1024w"
5     sizes="(max-width: 480px) 480px,
6            (max-width: 768px) 768px,
7            1024px"
8     alt="responsive image example">
```

In the srcset attribute, multiple image sources are provided along with their corresponding widths, denoted by w next to the image file path. This allows the browser to select the most appropriate version of the image to load based on the current viewport's width. The sizes attribute complements srcset by defining the conditions under which each image size is selected and the viewport segments they correspond to.

Integrating Webpack with responsive image strategies such as srcset significantly improves the performance and user experience of web applications by optimizing asset delivery. This setup allows developers to balance visual quality with load times, adapting to varying client-side conditions seamlessly.

Thus, once you have the infrastructure and process in place for sourcing and serving appropriately sized images per device or viewport conditions, the performance and responsiveness of your application can greatly increase, enhancing the overall user engagement and satisfaction.

8.9 Dynamic Asset Management with Import Expressions

Dynamic asset management is a technique that allows developers to load modules and assets conditionally or on demand, thereby improving the overall performance of a web application. This approach is particularly beneficial in scenarios where the application size is substantial, and not all assets are required immediately upon the application's initial load. Webpack facilitates dynamic asset management through the use of import expressions.

Import expressions, leveraging the promise-based `import()` function, allow for the dynamic resolution and loading of modules and assets. This method is advantageous over static imports as it enables more granular control over resource loading, resulting in a more efficient usage of network and system resources.

To implement dynamic asset management using import expressions, the following steps are typically followed:

- Identifying components or assets that are not required immediately and can be loaded lazily.

- Utilizing the `import()` function to import these components or assets on demand.

- Handling the returned promise to manage the asset once it is loaded.

An example of using an import expression to dynamically load an image asset is provided below:

```
1  // Dynamically import an image
2  function loadImage(imagePath) {
3    import(imagePath)
4      .then(image => {
```

```
 5      // Handle the successful loading of the image
 6      const imgElement = document.createElement('img');
 7      imgElement.src = image.default;
 8      document.body.appendChild(imgElement);
 9    })
10    .catch(error => {
11      // Handle any errors in loading the image
12      console.error('Error loading the image:', error);
13    });
14  }
15
16  // Example usage
17  loadImage('./path/to/image.jpg');
```

This example demonstrates the loading of an image file dynamically based on a given path. The import() function returns a promise, which is then resolved to obtain the module (in this case, the image file). Upon successful loading, an image element is created, its source set to the loaded image, and finally appended to the document body.

Utilizing import expressions introduces several benefits:

- **Improved Initial Load Performance:** By loading assets only when they are needed, the initial load time of the application can be significantly reduced.

- **Bandwidth Optimization:** Conditional loading of assets ensures that only the necessary resources are loaded, optimizing the usage of network bandwidth.

- **Enhanced User Experience:** A faster initial load time contributes to a smoother and more responsive user experience.

Dynamic asset management, facilitated by import expressions, represents a powerful optimization technique within the arsenal of a Webpack developer. By strategically applying this approach, developers can achieve a fine balance between performance and resource availability, tailoring the loading strategy to the specific needs of the application and its users.

8.10   Caching Assets for Better Performance

Caching is a technique used to temporarily store copies of files so that they can be accessed more quickly. In web development, caching is crucial for enhancing an application's performance, particularly in terms of load times. Webpack offers various mechanisms to implement caching, ensuring that assets like images, JS, and CSS files are efficiently served to the client.

- **Hashing**: Webpack can append a unique hash to the filename of each asset. This hash changes only when the content of the asset changes, which helps in invalidating the browser cache when the asset is updated. This is achieved using Webpack's output filename and chunkFilename options.

- **Cache Control Headers**: These HTTP headers are used by web servers to determine how, and for how long, to cache the website content. Developers can configure their web servers to include cache-control headers, specifying max-age, and other directives for caching strategies.

- **Service Workers**: They allow for fine-grained control over asset caching and serving. Service workers can programmatically manage a cache of responses, enabling complex caching strategies such as cache first, network first, or network with cache fallback.

Implementing caching with Webpack requires a concrete strategy tailored to the application's needs. Below are detailed examples of how to implement these caching strategies.

Hashing

To enable hashing in Webpack, adjust the 'output' configuration in webpack.config.js as follows:

```
1  output: {
2     filename: '[name].[contenthash].js',
```

```
3     chunkFilename: '[id].[contenthash].chunk.js'
4  }
```

This configuration ensures that each bundle generated by Webpack will have a unique hash based on its content. When an asset changes, its hash changes, prompting browsers to download the new version.

Cache Control Headers

Configuring cache control headers typically involves adjustments on the server. For example, when using an Apache server, one can add directives to the .htaccess file like so:

```
1  <FilesMatch ".(js|css|jpg|png)$">
2     Header set Cache-Control "max-age=604800, public"
3  </FilesMatch>
```

This configuration sets a max-age of one week for JS, CSS, and image files, instructing the browser to cache these files for that duration.

Service Workers

Integrating service workers for asset caching involves registering a service worker script in your application and then defining the caching strategies within that script. Here is a simple example of registering a service worker:

```
1  if ('serviceWorker' in navigator) {
2     window.addEventListener('load', () => {
3        navigator.serviceWorker.register('/service-worker.js')
4        .then(registration => {
5           console.log('SW registered: ', registration);
6        })
7        .catch(registrationError => {
8           console.log('SW registration failed: ', registrationError);
9        });
10    });
11 }
```

Within the service-worker.js, you might implement a simple cache-first strategy as follows:

```
1  self.addEventListener('fetch', event => {
```

```
2        event.respondWith(
3            caches.match(event.request)
4            .then(response => {
5                return response || fetch(event.request);
6            })
7        );
8    });
```

This code checks the cache for a matching request before attempting to fetch it from the network, providing a faster response for cached assets.

Effective caching is key to optimizing web application performance. By strategically employing hashing, cache control headers, and service workers, developers can ensure that their Webpack-built applications load quickly and efficiently, enhancing the user experience.

8.11   Asset Modules: Type Configurations

In this section, we discuss the configurations for asset modules, a Webpack feature that simplifies the inclusion and management of assets in a bundle. Asset modules eliminate the need for additional loaders for importing assets like images, fonts, and SVGs by providing a built-in mechanism to handle these file types directly.

Asset modules are categorized into four types based on the nature of asset handling: 'asset/resource', 'asset/inline', 'asset/source', and 'asset'. Each type serves a specific purpose and can be configured in the Webpack configuration file. Understanding these configurations allows developers to optimize asset management according to their project needs.

- `asset/resource` emits a separate file and exports the URL. It behaves similarly to `file-loader`. This type is ideal for handling assets like images and fonts that must be referenced via a URL.

- `asset/inline` exports a data URI of the asset. It functions similarly to `url-loader` with a small asset limit. This type is useful for small assets that should be inlined to reduce requests.

- asset/source exports the source code of the asset directly. This is similar to the behavior of raw-loader and is useful for importing asset data as a string.

- asset, which automatically chooses between exporting a data URI and emitting a separate file based on the file size, offers a balance between the asset/resource and asset/inline types. The default size limit for this decision can be configured, but it defaultly follows Webpack's default setting.

To configure an asset module type in Webpack, modify the module.rules array in your Webpack configuration file. The following example demonstrates configuring Webpack to use asset/resource for image files:

```
1   module.exports = {
2      module: {
3         rules: [
4            {
5               test: /\.(png|svg|jpg|jpeg|gif)$/i,
6               type: 'asset/resource',
7            },
8         ],
9      },
10  };
```

In this configuration, any import of an image file with extensions .png, .svg, .jpg, .jpeg, or .gif will automatically be handled as an asset/resource, emitting a separate file and exporting the URL to that file.

Advanced configuration options also exist, such as setting a custom output directory for emitted files or specifying a custom naming convention. For instance, one could customize the output path and file-names of assets using the generator property:

```
1   module.exports = {
2      module: {
3         rules: [
4            {
5               test: /\.(png|svg|jpg|jpeg|gif)$/i,
6               type: 'asset/resource',
7               generator: {
8                  filename: 'images/[hash][ext][query]',
9               },
10           },
```

226

```
11        ],
12      },
13  };
```

Here, [hash][ext][query] will generate files in an 'images' directory with their original extensions, a unique hash to prevent caching issues, and any original query parameters preserved. This level of customization ensures that asset handling can be finely tuned to meet the specific demands of each project.

Understanding and utilizing asset module types allows for more flexible and efficient management of assets within Webpack. By selecting the appropriate type and applying detailed configuration options, developers can significantly optimize asset loading and improve the overall performance and maintainability of their web applications.

8.12 Best Practices for Asset Management and Delivery

In the domain of web development, efficient management and delivery of assets are pivotal for enhancing the performance of web applications. This section delineates best practices that developers should adhere to when managing and delivering assets such as images, fonts, and other static content within a Webpack configuration.

- **Use Versioning for Cache Busting:** Assets should be versioned to facilitate cache busting. This can be achieved by appending a unique identifier to filenames during the build process. Webpack can automate this process through the use of hash-based naming.

```
1  module.exports = {
2    output: {
3      filename: '[name].[contenthash].js',
4      path: path.resolve(__dirname, 'dist')
5    }
6  };
```

- **Optimize Images Before Bundling:** Images should be optimized for the web before they are bundled with your application. This includes compression and resizing according to the requirements of the application. Tools and plugins such as `ImageMinimizerPlugin` can be configured within Webpack for this purpose.

```
1  module.exports = {
2      plugins: [
3          new ImageMinimizerPlugin({
4              minimizerOptions: {
5                  plugins: [
6                      ['jpegtran', { progressive: true }],
7                      ['optipng', { optimizationLevel: 5 }]
8                  ]
9              }
10         })
11     ]
12 };
```

- **Lazy Load Images:** Images that are not critical at the initial load time should be lazy loaded. This significantly reduces the initial load time and conserves bandwidth. Webpack supports lazy loading through dynamic imports.

- **Employ CDN for Asset Delivery:** Using a Content Delivery Network (CDN) for serving static assets can significantly enhance the speed of content delivery across the globe. When configuring assets in Webpack, it's beneficial to specify the CDN URL in the production environment configuration.

```
1  module.exports = {
2      output: {
3          publicPath: process.env.NODE_ENV === 'production'
4              ? 'https://your-cdn-url.com/'
5              : '/'
6      }
7  };
```

- **Configure Asset Modules Efficiently:** Webpack 5 introduced asset modules which enable developers to incorporate different types of assets directly into the bundle. Correctly configuring these modules by setting the right type (`asset/resource`, `asset/inline`, or `asset/source`) for each asset type ensures optimal bundling and delivery.

- **Use Appropriate Loaders for Fonts and SVGs:** For handling fonts and SVGs, ensure that the appropriate loaders are set up in the Webpack configuration. This facilitates better handling and optimization of these asset types, contributing to smaller bundle sizes and improved performance.

- **Implement Responsive Images with `srcset`:** Utilizing the `srcset` attribute in `img` tags enables the browser to select the most appropriate image size, leading to faster loading times and reduced bandwidth usage for devices with different screen resolutions.

- **Practice Code Splitting:** Code splitting allows for splitting the codebase into smaller chunks that can be loaded on demand or in parallel, drastically reducing the initial load time. Webpack facilitates code splitting through dynamic imports.

```
1  import(/* webpackChunkName: "my-chunk-name" */ 'path/to/myModule').
       then((module) => {
2      // Use module here
3  });
```

Following these best practices will significantly influence the efficiency of asset management and delivery in Webpack, thereby enhancing the performance and user experience of the web application.

Chapter 9

Setting Up a Development Environment with Webpack

Setting up an efficient development environment is crucial for a productive coding workflow, and this chapter focuses on how Webpack can be configured to create such an environment. It walks through the setup of Webpack DevServer for local development, enabling features like hot module replacement for live content updates without page refreshes. The chapter also covers the integration of source maps for easier debugging, and the use of tools like ESLint for maintaining code quality. Additionally, it touches on integrating Webpack with various editors and IDEs, managing environment variables, and optimizing the development build for speed. By the end of this chapter, readers will have a thorough understanding of how to harness Webpack to streamline their development process, making it faster and more efficient.

9.1   Introduction   to   Development Environment Setup with Webpack

Setting up an efficient development environment is fundamental for any web developer looking to maintain a productive coding workflow. This necessity becomes glaringly apparent as projects grow in complexity and size. Webpack, a static module bundler for JavaScript applications, emerges as a pivotal tool in orchestrating this environment.   By bundling application assets, Webpack simplifies both development and production workflows.

A development environment setup with Webpack involves several key steps, each designed to enhance the developer's efficiency and the application's performance. To begin with, it is imperative to understand the role of Webpack in a modern web development landscape.   As a module bundler, Webpack takes modules with dependencies and generates static assets representing those modules. The beauty of Webpack lies in its ability to transform, bundle, or package almost any resource or asset, following the configured instructions.

The initial step in configuring a development environment with Webpack is the installation process. This involves installing Webpack itself along with the Webpack CLI (Command Line Interface). The installation can be executed with npm (Node Package Manager), as illustrated in the following command:

```
1   npm install webpack webpack-cli --save-dev
```

This command installs Webpack and the Webpack CLI as development dependencies for the project, ensuring they are not included in the production build. Following installation, the next crucial step is configuring Webpack.   This process is facilitated through the creation of a Webpack configuration file, typically named webpack.config.js, at the root of the project.   The configuration file is a commonJS module that exports an object with Webpack configuration properties:

```
1   const path = require('path');
2
3   module.exports = {
```

```
4    entry: './src/index.js',
5    output: {
6      filename: 'bundle.js',
7      path: path.resolve(__dirname, 'dist'),
8    },
9  };
```

In this basic configuration example, two key aspects of the setup are defined: the `entry` and the `output`. The `entry` property specifies the entry point file of the application from which Webpack begins its bundling process. The `output` property, on the other hand, defines the output file's name and location where the bundled JavaScript will be stored.

Significantly, this configuration merely scratches the surface of what Webpack can do. Webpack's true power and flexibility lie in its rich ecosystem of loaders and plugins, which enable processing of various types of assets, such as CSS, images, and more, as well as extending its functionality.

To recapitulate, setting up a development environment with Webpack lays the groundwork for a streamlined and efficient development process. From installation and basic configuration to leveraging loaders and plugins for asset management and enhancement, Webpack serves as a robust foundation for developing modern web applications. As further sections will demonstrate, additional configurations and tools, including Hot Module Replacement and source maps integration, can augment this setup, leading to an even more dynamic and efficient development workflow.

9.2 Installing Webpack DevServer for Local Development

To establish a local development environment using Webpack, the installation of Webpack DevServer is essential. This tool allows for the serving of your web application locally and updates the browser automatically whenever changes to the source code are made. The following steps meticulously detail the installation process and initial configuration of Webpack DevServer.

Begin by ensuring that Node.js and npm (Node Package Manager) are installed on your system. These are prerequisites as Webpack and Webpack DevServer are Node.js applications and are managed through npm. Verify their installation by executing the following commands in your terminal:

```
1   node --version
2   npm --version
```

Once Node.js and npm are confirmed to be installed, the next step is to initiate a new Node.js project if you haven't already done so. This is accomplished by creating a new directory for your project and running the command:

```
1   npm init -y
```

This command generates a default package.json file, which is used to manage project dependencies. With the Node.js project initialized, the installation of Webpack and Webpack DevServer can proceed. Run the following command to install both as development dependencies:

```
1   npm install --save-dev webpack webpack-cli webpack-dev-server
```

After the installation completes, the next step is configuring Webpack to use DevServer. This is achieved by creating a webpack.config.js file at the root of your project. Inside this configuration file, specify the entry point of your application and the output path. Additionally, include the DevServer configuration as shown below:

```
1   module.exports = {
2     entry: './src/index.js',
3     output: {
4       path: __dirname + '/dist',
5       filename: 'bundle.js'
6     },
7     devServer: {
8       contentBase: './dist',
9     },
10  };
```

The `contentBase` option indicates the directory from which the DevServer will serve the files. Usually, this will be your `dist` folder where the Webpack-generated files reside.

Finally, to simplify the process of starting the DevServer, modify the `scripts` section of your `package.json` file to include a custom script for launching the server:

```
1  "scripts": {
2    "start": "webpack serve --open"
3  }
```

By adding this script, starting the DevServer is now as simple as running the command:

```
1  npm start
```

Upon execution, Webpack DevServer will start, and your default web browser will open automatically to the URL where your application is being served, typically `http://localhost:8080`. Now, any change made to the source code will be instantly reflected in the browser, significantly enhancing the development workflow by providing immediate feedback.

The installation and configuration of Webpack DevServer integrally streamline the development process, facilitating a highly efficient and productive coding environment. Following the outlined steps ensures that developers can leverage the full potential of Webpack DevServer for local development.

9.3 Configuring Hot Module Replacement for Instant Feedback

Hot Module Replacement (HMR) stands as a pivotal feature in modern web development, streamlining the development workflow by enabling live updates to the browser without a full page reload. This section delves into the configuration of Hot Module Replacement using Webpack, which promotes a more efficient and less disruptive coding experience.

The initial step requires the integration of Webpack DevServer, which provides a robust foundation for serving the application during development. To activate HMR, it is necessary to tweak both the Webpack configuration file and the development server setup. The process outlined below highlights the essential steps to configure HMR successfully:

- To commence, ensure that Webpack and Webpack DevServer are installed in your project. If not already installed, they can be added via npm or yarn.

```
1   npm install --save-dev webpack webpack-dev-server
```

- Within your `webpack.config.js` file, incorporate the `HotModuleReplacementPlugin` provided by Webpack. This plugin is instrumental in enabling HMR.

```
1   const webpack = require('webpack');
2
3   module.exports = {
4     // ...other configurations
5     plugins: [
6       new webpack.HotModuleReplacementPlugin(),
7     ],
8   };
```

- Modify the `devServer` configuration in `webpack.config.js` to activate HMR by setting the `hot` property to true.

```
1   devServer: {
2     contentBase: './dist',
3     hot: true,
4   },
```

- In your application's entry point or a high level module, implement the logic to accept updates for the modules that are to be hot reloaded.

```
1   if (module.hot) {
2     module.hot.accept('./myModule.js', function() {
3       // Callback for when the myModule.js or its dependencies are updated
4     });
5   }
```

- Finally, run the Webpack DevServer with the configuration tailored to utilize HMR. This can be done by adding a script to your package.json or running a command directly in the terminal.

```
1   npm run dev // Assuming "dev" script is configured to start Webpack
        DevServer
```

With these steps completed, HMR should be operational within your development environment, offering instant feedback by updating modules in the browser as changes are made in the codebase. It is important to test the configuration by making modifications to your source files; observing that updates are reflected in the browser without a full page reload verifies the successful setup of HMR.

For complex setups or troubleshooting HMR functionality, consult the official Webpack documentation which provides in-depth guidance and various scenarios for HMR integration. Remember, efficient tooling is a cornerstone of productive development practices, and configuring HMR with Webpack significantly contributes to such an environment.

9.4 Using Source Maps for Effective Debugging

The concept of source maps is not new, but its application in modern web development, especially with tools like Webpack, has become imperative for an effective debugging process. Source maps serve as bridges that link the transformed, often minified, version of your code back to its original state. This linkage is essential when debugging applications built with Webpack, where code is often concatenated, minified, and transformed in ways that make the original source difficult to recognize.

When you enable source maps in your Webpack configuration, Webpack generates files that map the transformed code back to the original source code. This means that when an error occurs, the browser's developer tools can display the file names and line numbers relevant to the original source, not the transformed code, making it significantly easier to identify and fix issues.

To configure Webpack to generate source maps, the `devtool` property in the Webpack configuration file must be set. Webpack offers several options for the `devtool` setting, each with its trade-offs in terms of build speed and quality of the source maps. The following code snippet demonstrates how to enable a commonly used source map setting:

```
1  module.exports = {
2    entry: './src/index.js',
3    output: {
4      filename: 'bundle.js',
5      path: __dirname + '/dist',
6    },
7    devtool: 'source-map',
8  };
```

In this configuration, the `'source-map'` option is used for the devtool property, signaling Webpack to generate external source map files. This choice provides a balance between build performance and the quality of the source maps. Though this option may slow down the build process slightly, the benefits in debugging efficiency are worth the trade-off for most development scenarios.

It's important to note that the inclusion of source maps in the production environment should be carefully considered due to potential impacts on performance and exposure of source code. For production builds, you might opt for a more compressed source map option or omit them entirely:

```
1  // Production webpack.config.js
2  module.exports = {
3    // Other configurations...
4    devtool: 'nosources-source-map', // Minimizes source code exposure
5  };
```

This setting, `'nosources-source-map'`, creates source maps that do not include the original source code. It allows the browser's developer tools to show code structure and line numbers without revealing the actual source code, striking a balanced compromise for production environments.

When it comes to analyzing the output and verifying the success of your source maps, you can use the browser's development tools. For example, in Google Chrome, opening the Developer Tools and navigating to the Sources tab reveals a tree structure on the left side, where you can find your original source code files, neatly separated and accessible for debugging, just as they were before the build process.

```
Uncaught TypeError: Cannot read property 'foo' of undefined
    at main.js:1:123456
```

With source maps enabled, rather than the cryptic `main.js:1:123456`, the error would refer directly to the file and line number in your original source code, making debugging a much more straightforward task.

To sum up, the integration of source maps into your Webpack configuration is a critical step towards efficient debugging. By properly understanding and employing this tool, developers can save time and energy when troubleshooting and refining their code, leading to a smoother and more productive development workflow.

9.5   Integrating Webpack with Visual Studio Code

Visual Studio Code (VS Code) is a popular Integrated Development Environment (IDE) that supports a wide range of programming languages and tools, including Webpack. Integrating Webpack with VS Code can significantly enhance the development workflow by providing instant access to build and debug tools within the IDE. This section details the steps and configurations required to achieve a seamless integration of Webpack with VS Code.

To begin with, make sure that Webpack and Webpack CLI are installed in your project. If not already installed, they can be added by running the following command in your project directory:

```
npm install --save-dev webpack webpack-cli
```

The next step involves configuring VS Code to recognize Webpack's build tasks. This can be accomplished by creating a tasks.json file within the .vscode directory of your project. The tasks.json file should include definitions for various Webpack commands you wish to run from within VS Code. Here is an example configuration that defines a build task:

```
{
    "version": "2.0.0",
    "tasks": [
        {
            "label": "webpack: build",
            "type": "shell",
            "command": "npx",
            "args": [
                "webpack",
                "--config",
                "./webpack.config.js"
            ],
            "group": {
                "kind": "build",
                "isDefault": true
            },
            "problemMatcher": [],
            "presentation": {
                "reveal": "always",
                "panel": "shared"
            }
        }
    ]
}
```

This task configuration allows developers to execute Webpack's build process directly from VS Code by leveraging the Command Palette (Ctrl+Shift+P) and selecting the "Run Task" option, followed by "webpack: build".

In order to enhance the development experience, it is advisable to install the Webpack extension for VS Code. This extension provides features such as syntax highlighting for Webpack configuration files and snippets for common configurations, thus simplifying the process of writing and maintaining Webpack configurations.

Furthermore, integrating source map support is crucial for

debugging the bundled files efficiently. Ensure that your webpack.config.js includes the devtool option set to a mode compatible with VS Code, such as 'source-map':

```
1  module.exports = {
2      // Other config options...
3      devtool: 'source-map',
4      // Remaining config...
5  };
```

The integration of ESLint into the Webpack and VS Code setup can significantly improve the code quality by enforcing consistent coding standards. This can be achieved by installing ESLint as a VS Code extension and configuring it to run as a pre-loader in webpack.config.js:

```
1  module: {
2      rules: [
3          {
4              test: /\.js$/,
5              exclude: /node_modules/,
6              use: ["babel-loader", "eslint-loader"]
7          }
8      ]
9  }
```

Lastly, to streamline your development workflow further, consider using VS Code's integrated terminal to run Webpack DevServer. This provides a single-window solution for editing code, executing builds, and monitoring output.

In summary, the integration of Webpack with Visual Studio Code can tremendously accelerate the development process by bringing the power of Webpack's build and debug functionalities directly into the IDE. The configurations and tips provided in this section are aimed at setting up a solid foundation for this integration, enabling developers to focus more on coding and less on switching between tools.

9.6   Setting Up ESLint for Code Quality and Consistency

Ensuring the quality and consistency of code in a project is paramount, and ESLint serves as an indispensable tool in achieving this objective. ESLint is a static code analysis tool for identifying problematic patterns found in JavaScript code. Its flexibility allows developers to configure rules according to their project's standards, thereby maintaining code quality and consistency across the development team. This section delineates the process of integrating ESLint into a Webpack-based development environment.

Firstly, the inclusion of ESLint in a project necessitates its installation. This is accomplished through npm, Node.js's package manager. The installation command is as follows:

```
1   npm install eslint --save-dev
```

Following ESLint's installation, the next step involves initializing ES-Lint in the project. This is achieved by running the `eslint --init` command, which prompts a series of questions concerning the configuration of ESLint. These questions pertain to the coding conventions and environments that the project will adhere to. For projects that are setup with Webpack, selecting "To check syntax, find problems, and enforce code style" offers a comprehensive setup.

```
1   eslint --init
```

Subsequent to configuration, integrating ESLint with Webpack demands the use of the `eslint-loader`. This loader allows Webpack to process code with ESLint before bundling. To install `eslint-loader`, the following command is used:

```
1   npm install eslint-loader --save-dev
```

Incorporating the `eslint-loader` into Webpack's configuration is performed within the `webpack.config.js` file. The loader is specified in the module rules, as seen in the code snippet below:

```
1   module: {
```

```
 2    rules: [
 3        {
 4            test: /\.js$/,
 5            exclude: /node_modules/,
 6            use: {
 7                loader: "eslint-loader",
 8                options: {
 9                    // Automatically fix minor issues
10                    fix: true
11                }
12            }
13        }
14    ]
15  }
```

The configuration snippet specifies that `eslint-loader` should process files with a '.js' extension, excluding any files within the `node_modules` directory. The `fix` option is set to `true` to enable ESLint's automatic correction of code style violations where feasible.

For projects that leverage modern JavaScript features or frameworks such as React, additional configuration may be needed. This involves installing the appropriate ESLint plugins and adding them to the ESLint configuration file (`.eslintrc`). For instance, to support JSX syntax used in React, the `eslint-plugin-react` package is required.

```
 1  npm install eslint-plugin-react --save-dev
```

Subsequently, the plugin is added to the `.eslintrc` file as shown below:

```
 1  {
 2      "plugins": [
 3          "react"
 4      ],
 5      "rules": {
 6          // React specific linting rules
 7      }
 8  }
```

ESLint's integration with Webpack enhances the development workflow by ensuring that all JavaScript code conforms to specified guidelines, thus improving code quality and consistency. Additionally, ESLint's flexibility in terms of configuration allows it to adapt to various coding styles and project requirements, making it an invaluable tool for projects of any scale.

9.7   Working with Babel for ES6+ Support

Working with modern JavaScript often involves using features from ES6 (ECMAScript 2015) and beyond, which brings enhanced syntax for better coding practices. However, not all browsers fully support these newer specifications. This issue makes Babel an indispensable tool within the development environment when utilizing Webpack. Babel is a JavaScript compiler that converts modern JavaScript (ES6+) code into a backwards compatible version that can be executed in current and older browsers or environments.

To integrate Babel with Webpack, the initial step involves installing the necessary packages. The core package is `babel-loader`, which allows Webpack to process JavaScript files using Babel. Alongside `babel-loader`, the `@babel/core` package, which is Babel's main dependency, and the `@babel/preset-env` package, a collection of Babel plugins that enables support for the latest JavaScript syntax, are also required.

```
1   npm install --save-dev babel-loader @babel/core @babel/preset-env
```

Upon successful installation, the next step is to configure Webpack to use `babel-loader` for JavaScript file processing. This is achieved by modifying the Webpack configuration file (`webpack.config.js`) to include a module rule for JavaScript files. The configuration specifies that all files with a `.js` extension should be processed by `babel-loader`, excluding the `node_modules` directory to speed up the build process.

```
1   module.exports = {
2     module: {
3       rules: [
4         {
5           test: /\.js$/,
6           exclude: /node_modules/,
7           use: {
8             loader: 'babel-loader',
9             options: {
```

```
10          presets: ['@babel/preset-env']
11        }
12      }
13    }
14  ]
15  }
16 };
```

The `options` field within the loader configuration specifies that `@babel/preset-env` should be used. This preset allows Babel to compile JavaScript code based on the target environment, which could be a specific set of browsers or versions thereof. By default, Babel with `@babel/preset-env` targets a broad range of environments, ensuring the compiled code is as compatible as possible.

For projects that require specific browser support, the `.browserslistrc` file can be utilized to define target environments. This file works in tandem with `@babel/preset-env` to tailor the compilation process, resulting in code that is optimized for specified browsers or environments.

```
> 0.25%
not dead
```

In the given example, the target is set to browsers with a usage greater than 0.25

Furthermore, for projects leveraging the latest JavaScript features like async/await, which are part of the ES2017 specification, additional setup might be required. In such cases, the `@babel/plugin-transform-runtime` package can be introduced to enable these features without polluting the global scope or adding duplicate code across multiple files.

```
1 npm install --save-dev @babel/plugin-transform-runtime
```

This package is then added to the Babel configuration, specifically in the `plugins` array, to ensure these modern constructs are accurately transpiled, and runtime helpers are automatically included in the output code for features like async functions.

In summary, integrating Babel with Webpack empowers developers to write modern and more readable JavaScript code without worrying about compatibility issues. Through the setup of Babel with the `babel-loader`, `@babel/core`, and `@babel/preset-env`, along with optional configurations and plugins for specific use cases, a Webpack-based development environment can seamlessly incorporate the latest JavaScript features, enhancing both the development experience and the compatibility of the deployed applications.

9.8   Incorporating TypeScript in Your Webpack Setup

Incorporating TypeScript into a Webpack setup requires a systematic approach to ensure seamless integration and efficiency in development flow. TypeScript, a superset of JavaScript, offers static typing capabilities that can significantly enhance code quality and scalability.   By integrating TypeScript with Webpack, developers can leverage the strengths of both technologies to create robust web applications. This section outlines the necessary steps to configure TypeScript with Webpack, including installation of necessary packages, configuration of TypeScript, and fine-tuning the Webpack setup to work with TypeScript files.

The first step in incorporating TypeScript into a Webpack setup is to install the required packages. This includes TypeScript itself and the TypeScript loader for Webpack, which facilitates the processing of TypeScript files. The installation can be accomplished using the Node.js package manager (npm) with the following commands:

```
1   npm install --save-dev typescript ts-loader
```

After successfully installing these packages, the next step is to configure TypeScript by creating a `tsconfig.json` file in the root directory of the project. This configuration file specifies the compiler options and the files to be included in the project. A basic `tsconfig.json` file may look like this:

```
1   {
```

```
 2    "compilerOptions": {
 3      "outDir": "./dist/",
 4      "noImplicitAny": true,
 5      "module": "es6",
 6      "target": "es5",
 7      "jsx": "react",
 8      "allowJs": true
 9    },
10    "include": [
11      "./src/**/*"
12    ]
13  }
```

In this configuration, the "compilerOptions" section sets various options for the TypeScript compiler. The "outDir" option specifies the output directory for compiled files, while "noImplicitAny" enforces typing on all variables. The "module" and "target" options define the module system and ECMAScript target version, respectively. The "jsx" option is particularly important for projects using React, as it enables JSX support. Finally, the "include" array determines which files are included in the compilation process.

With the TypeScript configuration in place, the Webpack configuration must be adjusted to handle TypeScript files. This involves modifying the webpack.config.js file to include ts-loader in the module rules. The modified module rules section of the configuration file may look as follows:

```
1  module: {
2    rules: [
3      {
4        test: /\.tsx?$/,
5        use: 'ts-loader',
6        exclude: /node_modules/
7      }
8    ]
9  }
```

The rule depicted here tells Webpack to use ts-loader for all files with extensions .ts or .tsx, excluding those in the node_modules directory. The test property uses a regular expression to match file extensions, while the use property specifies the loader to process those files.

Integrating TypeScript into a Webpack setup significantly enhances the development workflow by providing static typing capabilities.

This process involves installing TypeScript and ts-loader, configuring TypeScript via the tsconfig.json file, and adjusting the Webpack configuration to include TypeScript files in the compilation process. Following these steps will enable developers to efficiently use TypeScript in Webpack-based projects, facilitating improved code quality and maintainability.

9.9   Automating Tasks with NPM Scripts

Automating repetitive tasks is a cornerstone of efficient development workflows. NPM scripts serve as a powerful and versatile tool in this regard, especially when configured in conjunction with Webpack. This section will elaborate on how to leverage NPM scripts to automate common operations such as building, testing, and starting the development server, thereby streamlining the development process.

NPM (Node Package Manager) scripts are essentially shortcuts that can be defined in the package.json file of a Node.js project. These scripts are capable of executing any command-line operation. When incorporating Webpack into your development environment, utilizing NPM scripts can facilitate not just the build and bundle processes but also enable more complex workflows with minimal effort.

To begin with, the package.json file needs to contain a "scripts" section where custom scripts are defined. The basic structure is shown below:

```
"scripts": {
  "start": "webpack serve --open",
  "build": "webpack --mode production",
  "test": "echo \"Error: no test specified\" && exit 1"
}
```

In the above script definitions:

- The start script runs Webpack DevServer, opening the application in the default web browser automatically. This is particularly useful for speeding up the development cycle by providing immediate feedback.

- The `build` script executes Webpack in production mode, which typically includes optimizations like minification and dead code elimination to ensure the output is as efficient as possible.

- The `test` script is a placeholder for running tests. It can be replaced with the actual command to run your project's test suite.

To run these scripts, you would use the NPM command line interface with the run command, followed by the script name. For instance, to execute the build script, you would type:

```
1  npm run build
```

The output of running this command might look like the following, indicating that Webpack has successfully bundled the application:

```
> webpack --mode production

Hash: a3b4c5d6e7
Version: webpack 4.44.1
Time: 512ms
Built at: 01/01/2021 12:00:00
     Asset       Size  Chunks            Chunk Names
 bundle.js    1.2 MiB       0  [emitted]  main
 Entrypoint main = bundle.js
 [...]
```

For more complex workflows, NPM scripts can also execute multiple commands in sequence or in parallel. This can be achieved by using the && operator for sequential execution or the & operator for parallel execution. For example, a script to build the project and then start the server could look like this:

```
1  "scripts": {
2    "build:start": "npm run build && npm run start"
3  }
```

By employing NPM scripts, developers can automate the execution of Webpack along with other tools, thereby significantly reducing manual intervention and making the development process both faster and more error-free. The flexibility and ease of use offered by NPM scripts make them an indispensable feature of modern web development workflows.

9.10   Managing Environment Variables for Development and Production

Managing environment variables effectively is crucial for distinguishing between development and production environments in any web application. This section will discuss the role of environment variables in a Webpack setup and how to configure them for different environments. Webpack allows the management of such variables through its DefinePlugin, enabling developers to define global constants during the compile time of the project.

To begin, let's introduce the concept of environment variables within the context of Webpack. Environment variables are key-value pairs that can influence the way running processes will behave on a computer. For instance, they can determine the database to connect to, API endpoints, or even dictate the level of logging to output.

```
1   const webpack = require('webpack');
2   const dotenv = require('dotenv');
3
4   dotenv.config();
5
6   module.exports = {
7     plugins: [
8       new webpack.DefinePlugin({
9         'process.env.API_URL': JSON.stringify(process.env.API_URL),
10      }),
11    ],
12  };
```

In the preceding code snippet, the dotenv library is used to load environment variables from a .env file into process.env, making them accessible throughout the application. The DefinePlugin then takes these variables and makes them available globally in your JavaScript code, allowing for conditions based on the current environment like:

```
1   if (process.env.NODE_ENV === 'production') {
2     console.log('Production mode');
3   } else {
4     console.log('Development mode');
5   }
```

It's imperative to differentiate between development and production environments for multiple reasons. Development environments typically require more verbose logging, different API endpoints, and features like hot module replacement, while production environments demand optimizations such as minification, caching strategies, and security enhancements.

Setting up separate .env files for development and production environments can greatly streamline this differentiation process. An example of such a setup would include a .env.development file for development environment variables and a .env.production file for production environment variables.

Webpack's ability to handle these environment variables through DefinePlugin and other mechanisms plays a pivotal role in maintaining the integrity and functionality of the application across different environments. Moreover, integrating these environment variables can be further optimized using additional NPM scripts defined in your package.json file, targeting different environments like so:

```
1  "scripts": {
2    "start": "webpack serve --env development",
3    "build": "webpack --env production"
4  }
```

In this configuration, running npm start will trigger the development environment setup, while npm run build will cater to the production environment. This level of control is crucial for tailoring the application's behavior and performance to suit the needs of each environment effectively.

Finally, maintaining a clear and organized approach to managing environment variables with Webpack promotes a scalable and maintainable codebase. It not only improves the development experience but also ensures that the application runs optimally in production, catering to its intended audience successfully.

9.11   Optimizing Development Workflow with Proxying API Requests

Optimizing a development workflow involves numerous elements, and an integral aspect is efficiently managing API requests during development. This section explicates the configuration of a proxy in Webpack DevServer, which directs API requests from the development server to a backend server. This technique is pivotal for circumventing cross-origin request issues and ensures a seamless development process.

To initiate the setup, the devServer property in the Webpack configuration file (webpack.config.js) needs to be modified. Within this property, the proxy key is specified, which is responsible for redirecting API requests. The following listing demonstrates the basic configuration:

```
module.exports = {
  // Other configurations...
  devServer: {
    proxy: {
      '/api': {
        target: 'http://localhost:3000',
        secure: false,
        changeOrigin: true,
        pathRewrite: { '^/api': '' },
      },
    },
  },
};
```

This configuration routes requests from the frontend application directing towards "/api" to a backend server hosted at "http://localhost:3000". The secure: false setting is typically used for development environments where SSL/TLS might not be in use, implying that HTTPS requests can be proxied over an insecure connection. The changeOrigin property alters the origin of the host header to match the target's host, curtailing potential host mismatch issues during proxying. Lastly, pathRewrite is used to remove the "/api" prefix from the request path before forwarding it to the backend, allowing for cleaner URL structures on both ends.

In certain scenarios, complex proxying rules are required to handle multiple backend services or to conditionally proxy requests. In such cases, proxy can be configured as an array of objects, each specifying distinct proxying rules:

```
devServer: {
  proxy: [
    {
      context: ['/api', '/other-service'],
      target: 'http://localhost:3000',
      changeOrigin: true,
    },
    {
      context: (pathName) => pathName.startsWith('/special-case'),
      target: 'http://localhost:5000',
      changeOrigin: true,
    },
  ],
},
```

Here, the first entry proxies requests targeting "/api" or "/other-service" to "http://localhost:3000". The second entry demonstrates a function-based context, allowing for more granular control over which requests to proxy. Using a function facilitates the implementation of logic to dynamically determine whether to proxy the request, based on the path.

Using a proxy in the development environment simplifies the interaction between the frontend and backend, removing the need for CORS (Cross-Origin Resource Sharing) configuration on the backend server for development purposes. Furthermore, it mirrors more closely the production environment where both frontend and backend resources might be served from the same origin, thereby reducing the discrepancies between development and production setups.

To summarize, configuring a proxy through Webpack DevServer is an effective strategy to enhance the development workflow, especially when working with APIs. It not only aids in avoiding common issues like CORS but also streamlines the development process by allowing developers to work on the frontend and backend concurrently with fewer interruptions.

9.12   Debugging   Webpack   Configuration Issues

Configuring Webpack can often be an intricate process fraught with potential for missteps, particularly when integrating multiple complex plugins or loaders. Given the modular nature of Webpack, the root cause of an issue can sometimes be elusive. This section will elucidate the common issues encountered when working with Webpack configurations and offer systematic approaches to debugging them.

Identifying Configuration Errors

One of the first steps in debugging involves identifying the specific type of problem you are facing. Here are common categories of issues:

- **Build Failures:** Compilation errors or Webpack failing to complete the build process.

- **Runtime Errors:** Problems that occur in the browser once the application is running, which can be related to incorrect bundle configuration.

- **Performance Issues:** Slow build times or an oversized final bundle can indicate misconfiguration or misuse of plugins and loaders.

Using Webpack's Built-in Logging

Webpack offers built-in verbosity options that can be incredibly helpful for pinpointing configuration issues. Setting the `stats` option in your Webpack configuration file to `'verbose'` will provide detailed information during the build process.

```
module.exports = {
    // ...
    stats: 'verbose',
};
```

254

This configuration directive instructs Webpack to output a comprehensive log of everything it does during the build process, potentially highlighting any misconfigurations.

Analyzing Build Errors and Warnings

When Webpack encounters an error or warning during the build, it attempts to describe the problem. However, the output can sometimes be cryptic. Critical to resolving these messages is locating the precise module or plugin where the issue arises. Consider this example error output:

```
ERROR in ./src/index.js
Module not found: Error: Can't resolve './missing-module'
in '/path/to/project/src'
```

This message indicates that Webpack could not resolve a module import in index.js. The typical resolution involves verifying the path and name of the imported module.

Leveraging Source Maps for Runtime Errors

For runtime errors, enabling source maps can be incredibly beneficial. Source maps provide a way to map the transformed and bundled code back to the original source code, making debugging significantly more straightforward. To enable source maps, add the following line to your Webpack configuration:

```
1  devtool: 'source-map',
```

With source-map enabled, browser developer tools will reference the original source code location of errors, rather than the bundled code.

Utilizing Webpack Analyze Tools

Several tools are available to analyze and visualize the content of Webpack bundles. One widely-used tool is webpack-bundle-analyzer. Installing and integrating this plugin into your Webpack configuration allows you to visualize bundle sizes, assisting in identifying large or unnecessary dependencies that could be contributing to performance issues.

```
1   const BundleAnalyzerPlugin = require('webpack-bundle-analyzer').
        BundleAnalyzerPlugin;
2
3   module.exports = {
4       // ...
5       plugins: [new BundleAnalyzerPlugin()]
6   };
```

By graphically representing the contents of the bundle, developers can make informed decisions about optimizing their application's load time.

Debugging Webpack configuration can be daunting due to the myriad of plugins, loaders, and options available. However, by methodically isolating the issue, utilizing Webpack's verbosity, and leveraging tools designed for analysis and debugging, developers can efficiently resolve configuration issues. It is critical to approach debugging with patience and systematically alter one aspect of the configuration at a time to decipher the precise cause of the problem.

Chapter 10

Advanced Topics: Webpack and the Modern JavaScript Ecosystem

This chapter delves into advanced topics that showcase Webpack's versatility and its integration within the modern JavaScript ecosystem. It explores how Webpack interacts with cutting-edge JavaScript frameworks, supports server-side rendering (SSR) for SEO and performance benefits, and facilitates code sharing through Module Federation. Additionally, the chapter addresses building Progressive Web Apps (PWAs) for enhanced offline experiences, optimizing large-scale applications, and internationalizing projects. It also discusses emerging trends in web development and anticipates the evolving role of Webpack. By engaging with these advanced topics, developers will be equipped with the knowledge to leverage Webpack in complex, modern web development scenarios, ensuring their projects are scalable, maintainable, and ahead of the curve.

10.1   Integrating   Webpack   with   Modern JavaScript Frameworks

Integrating Webpack with modern JavaScript frameworks is essential for developers aiming to streamline the build processes of their web applications. Webpack serves as a powerful module bundler, allowing for the management of dependencies, optimization of assets, and much more. This section will focus on the integration process of Webpack with popular frameworks such as React, Vue.js, and Angular, highlighting the specific configurations and practices that optimize their collaboration.

React Integration: React's ecosystem benefits significantly from Webpack's capabilities, particularly in handling JSX transformation and optimizing the development process with features like hot module replacement (HMR). To integrate Webpack with a React project, the following configurations are key:

```
const path = require('path');
const HtmlWebpackPlugin = require('html-webpack-plugin');

module.exports = {
  entry: './src/index.js',
  output: {
    path: path.resolve(__dirname, 'dist'),
    filename: 'bundle.js'
  },
  module: {
    rules: [
      {
        test: /\.(js|jsx)$/,
        exclude: /node_modules/,
        use: {
          loader: 'babel-loader',
          options: {
            presets: ['@babel/preset-react', '@babel/preset-env']
          }
        }
      }
    ]
  },
  plugins: [
    new HtmlWebpackPlugin({
      template: './src/index.html'
    })
  ],
  resolve: {
```

```
30    extensions: ['.js', '.jsx']
31  }
32 };
```

This configuration file sets the entry point, specifies the output, and includes rules for handling '.js' and '.jsx' files with 'babel-loader'. The HtmlWebpackPlugin is used to inject the bundle into the 'index.html'. The 'resolve' section ensures that imports without file extensions are properly handled.

Vue.js Integration: Webpack's integration with Vue.js streamlines single-file component (SFC) compilation, CSS extraction, and more. Essential to this setup is the 'vue-loader', a Webpack loader that allows the parsing and transpiling of Vue components. Example configuration:

```
1  const { VueLoaderPlugin } = require('vue-loader');
2  const path = require('path');
3
4  module.exports = {
5    entry: './src/main.js',
6    output: {
7      path: path.resolve(__dirname, 'dist'),
8      filename: 'bundle.js'
9    },
10   module: {
11     rules: [
12       {
13         test: /\.vue$/,
14         loader: 'vue-loader'
15       },
16       {
17         test: /\.css$/,
18         use: [
19           'vue-style-loader',
20           'css-loader'
21         ]
22       }
23     ]
24   },
25   plugins: [
26     new VueLoaderPlugin()
27   ]
28 };
```

The 'VueLoaderPlugin' is crucial as it enables 'vue-loader' to function properly. The configuration also demonstrates how to handle CSS files imported in Vue components, using 'vue-style-loader' and 'css-loader'.

Angular Integration: While Angular CLI abstracts away the need for manual Webpack configuration for many projects, understanding how to integrate Webpack can offer more control and optimization opportunities. A foundational aspect is the TypeScript compilation and Angular template loading. A simplified example includes:

```
1   const path = require('path');
2   const HtmlWebpackPlugin = require('html-webpack-plugin');
3
4   module.exports = {
5     entry: './src/main.ts',
6     output: {
7       path: path.resolve(__dirname, 'dist'),
8       filename: 'app.bundle.js'
9     },
10    module: {
11      rules: [
12        {
13          test: /\.tsx?$/,
14          loader: 'ts-loader',
15          exclude: /node_modules/
16        },
17        {
18          test: /\.html$/,
19          loader: 'html-loader'
20        }
21      ]
22    },
23    resolve: {
24      extensions: ['.ts', '.tsx', '.js']
25    },
26    plugins: [
27      new HtmlWebpackPlugin({
28        template: './src/index.html'
29      })
30    ]
31  };
```

The configuration specifies handling of TypeScript files ('.ts' and '.tsx') using 'ts-loader' and HTML files through 'html-loader'. The 'HtmlWebpackPlugin' is also utilized for template injection.

By customizing configurations to fit the needs of React, Vue.js, and Angular projects, developers can leverage Webpack to substantially enhance the development and deployment workflows. It is critical to understand the unique aspects of each framework to properly integrate Webpack. This ensures efficient builds and contributes to more maintainable and scalable web applications.

10.2 Server-Side Rendering (SSR) with Web-pack

Server-Side Rendering (SSR) is a technique that renders a client-side dynamic web page on the server and sends a fully rendered HTML to the client. This approach significantly improves the initial load time, aids in Search Engine Optimization (SEO), and enhances the overall user experience by displaying the web content without waiting for JavaScript to become interactive. Webpack, a powerful module bundler, plays a pivotal role in implementing SSR in modern web applications by bundling server-side scripts in a way that optimizes performance and compatibility.

Configuring Webpack for SSR: The first step is to create a separate Webpack configuration for the server. This configuration will differ from the client-side configuration primarily in the target, entry, and output fields.

```
const path = require('path');
const nodeExternals = require('webpack-node-externals');

module.exports = {
  target: 'node', // Ensures native node modules are not bundled
  entry: './src/server/index.js', // Server entry point
  output: {
    path: path.resolve(__dirname, 'dist'),
    filename: 'server.bundle.js'
  },
  externals: [nodeExternals()], // Avoids bundling external modules
  module: {
    rules: [
      {
        test: /\.js$/,
        use: 'babel-loader',
        exclude: /node_modules/,
      },
      {
        test: /\.css$/,
        use: 'ignore-loader'
      }
    ]
  }
};
```

The target: 'node' setting informs Webpack that the bundle will be used in a Node.js environment, allowing Node.js-specific

261

variables like `__dirname` to work correctly. The `nodeExternals()` function from the `webpack-node-externals` package tells Webpack to leave node_modules unbundled, significantly improving build time.

Integrating SSR with Express: After configuring Webpack to bundle server-side scripts, integrating SSR with an Express application involves serving the bundled server file. Here is an example of integrating SSR with an Express server:

```
 1  const express = require('express');
 2  const serverRenderer = require('./dist/server.bundle.js').default;
 3
 4  const app = express();
 5
 6  app.use(express.static('public')); // Serves static files
 7
 8  app.get('*', (req, res) => {
 9    serverRenderer(req, path, context => {
10      res.status(200).send(context.html);
11    });
12  });
13
14  const PORT = process.env.PORT || 3000;
15  app.listen(PORT, () => {
16    console.log(`Server is listening on port ${PORT}`);
17  });
```

This code snippet creates an Express application that serves static files from the `public` directory and uses the server-rendered content for all other routes. The `serverRenderer` function is responsible for generating the HTML content server-side and sending it as the response.

Benefits of SSR with Webpack:

- **SEO Optimization**: Server-rendered pages are fully readable to search engine crawlers, improving the visibility of the web application.

- **Improved Load Time**: Sending a fully rendered HTML page from the server accelerates the perceived load time since the user sees the content immediately.

- **Code Sharing**: Webpack's module federation features can be leveraged in SSR to share code between client and server bundles, reducing redundancy and improving maintainability.

Integrating SSR with Webpack offers considerable advantages for modern web applications by enhancing SEO, improving load times, and facilitating code sharing. A carefully configured Webpack setup ensures that server-side and client-side scripts are efficiently bundled, delivering a seamless integration between the server and client realms. As web development continues to evolve, techniques like SSR will remain essential for delivering high-performance, user-friendly web applications.

10.3 Module Federation: Sharing Code Between Multiple Webpack Bundles

Module Federation is a groundbreaking feature in Webpack that allows multiple independent builds to function together at runtime. This approach is particularly beneficial for microfrontend architectures, where various frontend applications, potentially developed by different teams using different technologies, need to share code or functionality seamlessly.

To understand Module Federation, we start by configuring a basic Module Federation setup. The key components of this setup involve specifying the 'ModuleFederationPlugin' within your Webpack configuration. This plugin is used to delineate the boundaries of shared modules, indicate which modules are being exposed by an application, and which remote modules an application intends to consume.

```
1  const ModuleFederationPlugin = require("webpack/lib/container/
       ModuleFederationPlugin");
2
3  module.exports = {
4    plugins: [
5      new ModuleFederationPlugin({
6        name: "app1",
7        library: { type: "var", name: "app1" },
8        filename: "remoteEntry.js",
9        exposes: {
10         './Module': './src/Module',
11       },
```

```
12      remotes: {
13        app2: "app2",
14      },
15      shared: ["react", "react-dom"],
16    }),
17  ],
18 };
```

In this configuration, 'app1' exposes a module located at
'./src/Module' and attempts to consume modules from 'app2'. The
'filename' property refers to the name of the build output that
serves as the entry point for the remote module. Note the use of
'shared' to indicate common dependencies like 'react' and
'react-dom', which helps to prevent duplication of these libraries
across bundles, optimizing load times and performance.

Remote applications or component libraries are consumed using dynamic imports, which enable asynchronous loading of code at runtime. Below is an example demonstrating how 'app1' might dynamically import a module from 'app2'.

```
1 (async () => {
2   const remoteModule = await import("app2/Module");
3   // Use the dynamically imported module
4 })();
```

It is crucial to understand that the code shared between applications
through Module Federation remains isolated within its runtime environment. This isolation ensures that shared modules do not inadvertently affect the global scope or interfere with the host application's
execution context.

During development, handling cross-domain module federation
requires configuring CORS (Cross-Origin Resource Sharing)
policies to ensure resources can be shared between different
domains securely. In production, proper domain and path
structures must be established to ensure federated modules are
accessible to consuming applications.

The ability to share live code between independently deployed applications offers significant advantages for scaling projects, improving
team autonomy, and reducing code duplication. However, it also introduces complexity in terms of dependency management and ver-

sioning. Careful consideration must be given to the version compatibility of shared modules to prevent runtime errors.

Applying Module Federation in a project allows for a more flexible architecture, enhancing the scalability and maintainability of large-scale applications. It fosters an environment where applications can stay modular and decoupled, even as they grow and evolve.

To summarize, Module Federation transforms the way applications are developed, deployed, and integrated in the modern web ecosystem. By enabling seamless code sharing and microfrontend architectures, it addresses numerous challenges faced by developers and organizations striving to deliver complex, robust web applications.

10.4 Building Progressive Web Apps (PWAs) with Webpack

Building Progressive Web Apps (PWAs) requires an understanding of several key principles, such as service workers, web app manifests, and strategies for offline functionality. Webpack, due to its extensible nature, offers an efficient way to bundle and optimize these elements, making the transition from traditional web applications to PWAs smooth and straightforward.

A PWA, in essence, is a web application that uses modern web capabilities to deliver a user experience similar to that of mobile apps. Key features of PWAs include reliability, performance, and engagement. These are achieved through service workers for offline support and cache management, web app manifests for adding the app to the home screen, and push notifications for user re-engagement.

Service Workers:

To start integrating service workers into your project using Webpack, first install 'workbox-webpack-plugin'. Workbox is a set of libraries and Node modules that make it easy to cache assets and take full advantage of features used to build Progressive Web Apps.

```
1  npm install workbox-webpack-plugin --save-dev
```

Following the installation, configure the plugin in your webpack.config.js file. This involves importing the plugin and adding an instance of it to the plugins array. The configuration below illustrates a basic setup.

```
1   const { GenerateSW } = require('workbox-webpack-plugin');
2
3   module.exports = {
4     // Other Webpack configurations
5     plugins: [
6       new GenerateSW({
7         clientsClaim: true,
8         skipWaiting: true,
9       })
10    ]
11  };
```

The GenerateSW plugin will generate a service worker file that precaches resources, making them accessible offline and speeding up subsequent visits.

Web App Manifest:

Creating a web app manifest involves defining a JSON file that provides information about the application (such as name, author, icon, and description) in a standardized format. Webpack can automate the injection of this manifest into your project using the WebpackPwaManifest plugin.

```
1   npm install webpack-pwa-manifest --save-dev
```

Once installed, include it in your webpack.config.js alongside other plugins. The configuration snippet below demonstrates how to incorporate the manifest into your Webpack build process.

```
1   const WebpackPwaManifest = require('webpack-pwa-manifest');
2
3   module.exports = {
4     // Other Webpack configurations
5     plugins: [
6       new WebpackPwaManifest({
7         name: 'Your App Name',
8         short_name: 'AppShortName',
9         description: 'Your App Description',
10        background_color: '#ffffff',
11        crossorigin: 'use-credentials', // Can be set to 'anonymous'
12        icons: [
13          {
14            src: path.resolve('src/assets/icon.png'),
```

```
15        sizes: [96, 128, 192, 256, 384, 512] // Multiple sizes
16      }
17    ]
18  })
19  ]
20 };
```

Incorporating these configurations in your Webpack setup effectively transforms your web application into a PWA, making it much more performant, reliable, and engaging.

Strategies for Offline Functionality:

Beyond caching assets, sophisticated offline functionality requires strategies for network requests. This can range from simple cache-first approaches to more complex strategies like network-first, stale-while-revalidate, or cache-only. Workbox provides straightforward ways to implement these strategies.

```
1 workbox.routing.registerRoute(
2   new RegExp('.*\.js'),
3   new workbox.strategies.NetworkFirst()
4 );
```

This example uses the NetworkFirst strategy for JavaScript files, ensuring that your application attempts to reach the network first before falling back to the cache. Similar patterns can be applied for CSS, images, and API requests, depending on the specific needs of your application.

To summarize, integrating PWAs with Webpack enhances the user experience by leveraging modern web technologies. Through careful configuration and the use of plugins like Workbox and WebpackPwaManifest, developers can efficiently turn a traditional web application into a Progressive Web App, with all the benefits of offline functionality, fast load times, and an engaging user interface.

10.5   Webpack and TypeScript: Advanced Typing and Bundling

In this section, we will discuss the integration of TypeScript with Webpack to enhance the development workflow for building robust web applications. TypeScript, a superset of JavaScript, brings strong typing to the flexible, but dynamically typed world of JavaScript, enabling developers to catch errors early in the development process. When combined with Webpack's comprehensive bundling capabilities, developers gain the tools necessary for producing highly optimized and error-free code.

To begin, setting up TypeScript with Webpack requires the inclusion of the TypeScript loader, which is responsible for compiling TypeScript (.ts) files into JavaScript (.js) files that the browser can interpret. This process can be initiated by installing the TypeScript loader, usually 'ts-loader' or 'awesome-typescript-loader', via npm or yarn. For demonstration purposes, the installation of 'ts-loader' is presented below:

```
1   npm install --save-dev typescript ts-loader
```

Following the installation, a TypeScript configuration file, 'tsconfig.json', must be created. This file is essential for specifying the compiler options required for the project. A simple 'tsconfig.json' may look like this:

```
1   {
2     "compilerOptions": {
3       "outDir": "./dist/",
4       "noImplicitAny": true,
5       "module": "es6",
6       "target": "es5",
7       "allowJs": true
8     }
9   }
```

Here, 'outDir' specifies the output directory for the compiled JavaScript files. The 'noImplicitAny' flag ensures that no implicit 'any' types are allowed, enforcing strict typing. The 'module' and 'target' options determine the module system and the ECMAScript target version, respectively.

Next, integrating TypeScript into the Webpack configuration involves adding the 'ts-loader' to the module rules and ensuring that '.ts' and '.tsx' (if using React) file extensions are resolved by Webpack. An example Webpack configuration snippet is as follows:

```
module.exports = {
  entry: './src/index.ts',
  module: {
    rules: [
      {
        test: /\.tsx?$/,
        use: 'ts-loader',
        exclude: /node_modules/,
      },
    ],
  },
  resolve: {
    extensions: ['.tsx', '.ts', '.js'],
  },
  output: {
    filename: 'bundle.js',
    path: path.resolve(__dirname, 'dist'),
  },
};
```

In this configuration, 'entry' specifies the entry point file, and the module rules apply 'ts-loader' to all files matching the '.tsx¿ pattern, thus handling both '.ts' and '.tsx' files. The 'resolve' property's 'extensions' array allows Webpack to process files with '.ts', '.tsx', and '.js' extensions, in that order.

Properly integrating TypeScript with Webpack also involves leveraging source maps for easier debugging. This can be achieved by setting the 'devtool' option in the Webpack configuration to a value like 'inline-source-map'. This ensures that when errors occur, the TypeScript source files are referenced in the browser's developer tools, not the compiled JavaScript files.

```
devtool: 'inline-source-map',
```

Additionally, Advanced TypeScript typing features, such as

Interfaces and Enums, can be seamlessly used within the Webpack framework, allowing developers to define clear and concise types for their data structures and constants. TypeScript's strong typing system not only improves developer productivity through features like auto-completion but also significantly reduces runtime errors by catching them at compile time.

Integrating TypeScript with Webpack requires careful configuration but yields substantial benefits by combining TypeScript's advanced typing and error checking capabilities with Webpack's powerful module bundling. This synergy enables developers to build more maintainable, scalable, and error-free web applications.

10.6   Optimizing Webpack for Large Projects

Optimizing Webpack configurations for large-scale projects is crucial to ensure fast build times, efficient resource management, and an optimized final bundle. This section provides detailed strategies and best practices for achieving optimal performance in large projects.

Code Splitting

One of the first steps in optimizing a Webpack bundle for large projects is to implement code splitting. This technique allows you to split your code into smaller chunks, which can be loaded on demand or in parallel, reducing the initial load time of your application.

```
1   splitChunks: {
2     chunks: 'all',
3     maxInitialRequests: Infinity,
4     minSize: 0,
5     cacheGroups: {
6       vendor: {
7         test: /[\\/]node_modules[\\/]/,
8         name(module) {
9           const packageName = module.context.match(/[\\/]node_modules[\\/](.*?)
                 ([\\/]|$)/)[1];
10          return `npm.${packageName.replace('@', '')}`;
11        },
12      },
```

```
13    },
14    }
```

This configuration enables more aggressive splitting of the bundle by creating a chunk for each npm package used in your project, significantly improving caching and reducing the size of the initial bundle loaded by users.

Lazy Loading

Lazy loading is a technique that delays the loading of non-critical resources at page load time. Instead, these resources are loaded at the point they are needed, which can significantly reduce the initial load time.

```
1    const AsyncComponent = React.lazy(() => import('./AsyncComponent'));
```

This example uses React's lazy function to dynamically import a component. The component is only loaded when it is rendered, which can greatly improve the performance of your application.

Tree Shaking

Tree shaking is a term commonly used in the context of JavaScript for dead-code elimination. It relies on the static structure of ES2015 module syntax, i.e., 'import' and 'export'. Configuring Webpack for tree shaking involves ensuring that your code is free of side-effects and using the 'production' mode to enable minification and dead code removal.

```
1    module.exports = {
2      mode: 'production',
3    };
```

Caching

Caching can dramatically speed up build times in large projects. Webpack provides several caching mechanisms, which can be utilized to cache the output of loaders and plugins.

```
cache: {
  type: 'filesystem',
  buildDependencies: {
    config: [__filename],
  },
}
```

This configuration enables filesystem caching, which caches the output of loaders and reduces build times on subsequent builds.

Parallelization

Leveraging multi-core processors can significantly reduce build times. Webpack's 'thread-loader' can be used to offload expensive loaders to a worker pool.

```
{
  test: /\.js$/,
  exclude: /node_modules/,
  use: ['thread-loader', 'babel-loader'],
}
```

Adding 'thread-loader' before expensive loaders like 'babel-loader' can reduce compile times by parallelizing the workload.

Monitoring and Analysis

Continuously monitoring and analyzing the bundle size is critical for maintaining optimal performance. Webpack's 'BundleAnalyzerPlugin' provides a powerful visualization of what's included in your bundles, making it easier to identify and eliminate unnecessary dependencies.

```
const BundleAnalyzerPlugin = require('webpack-bundle-analyzer').
    BundleAnalyzerPlugin;

module.exports = {
  plugins: [
    new BundleAnalyzerPlugin(),
  ],
};
```

By incorporating these optimization strategies, Webpack can be effectively configured to handle the demands of large-scale projects, ensuring that your bundles are efficiently managed and optimized for both development and production environments.

10.7 Implementing   Internationalization (i18n) and Localization

Implementing internationalization (i18n) and localization within a Webpack-enabled project is pivotal for reaching a global audience. This section elucidates the methodologies and Webpack configurations essential for incorporating i18n and localization, thereby making your web applications accessible and functional for users across different geographies and languages.

The journey starts with understanding the core difference between internationalization and localization. Internationalization entails designing a web application in a manner that it can adapt to various languages and regions without requiring significant changes. Localization, on the other hand, involves the actual process of adapting your application for a specific language or region, including translating text and adjusting functional elements to local preferences.

Setting Up i18n with Webpack:

Initially, it is requisite to incorporate libraries that enable i18n functionality within your project. Libraries such as `i18next` and `react-i18next` (for React projects) are widely recognized for their efficacy in this domain. Following the installation, the next significant step is to configure Webpack to work seamlessly with your i18n library.

The `webpack.config.js` file is where most of the configuration takes place:

```
1   const path = require('path');
2
3   module.exports = {
4       // Existing configuration
5       module: {
```

```
 6        rules: [
 7            {
 8                test: /\.json$/,
 9                loader: 'i18next-resource-store-loader',
10                include: [
11                    path.resolve(__dirname, 'src/locales')
12                ],
13                options: {
14                    functionName: 'i18next.t'
15                }
16            },
17        ],
18    },
19    // Other configurations
20 };
```

In this configuration, the `i18next-resource-store-loader` is utilized to bundle your locale files with Webpack, thus enabling smooth integration with the i18next library. It's vital to place your locale files under a designated directory, such as `src/locales` in this instance, allowing Webpack to accurately process and include them in your bundle.

Localization File Structure:

A systematic approach to organizing your locale files is imperative for effective localization. Typically, a locale directory may resemble the following structure:

- `/locales`
    - `/en`
        * `translation.json`
    - `/de`
        * `translation.json`

Each subdirectory within the `locales` directory pertains to a different language (e.g., en for English, de for German), and contains language-specific translation files.   Leveraging JSON format for these files enables a straightforward key-value pairing for text references and their corresponding translations.

Dynamic Locale Loading:

For projects expecting to support numerous languages or requiring regular updates to translation content, dynamically loading locale resources becomes essential. Dynamic loading mitigates the initial load time by fetching only the necessary language files based on the user's preference or browser settings. Webpack's code splitting feature can be ingeniously applied to achieve this:

```
1   import(`./locales/${language}/translation.json`)
2     .then(translations => {
3       i18next.addResourceBundle(language, 'translation', translations);
4     });
```

This snippet demonstrates how you can dynamically import a translation file based on the variable language. Webpack interprets the import statement as a cue to split off this segment of your bundle, hence performing code splitting automatically.

Integrating internationalization and localization into your Webpack projects is a substantial step towards creating inclusive, globally-aware web applications. By leveraging libraries like i18next, structuring localization files appropriately, and utilizing Webpack's dynamic loading capabilities, developers can efficiently cater to a worldwide audience. This not only enhances user experience across different locales but also significantly broadens the potential user base for your web applications.

10.8 Automating Critical CSS Inlining

Automating Critical CSS Inlining involves extracting and inline the CSS necessary to render the above-the-fold content of a webpage. This technique is highly beneficial for improving the performance of web applications by reducing the time to first paint (TTFP) and ensuring a faster user experience. Webpack, equipped with various plugins and loaders, can automate this process effectively, ensuring that only the essential CSS is loaded initially.

To implement Critical CSS Inlining in a project using Webpack, the html-webpack-plugin and critical package are commonly utilized. Here is an example workflow for automating the process:

Firstly, ensure that the project has the necessary dependencies installed by running:

```
npm install --save-dev html-webpack-plugin critical
```

Next, configure Webpack to use `html-webpack-plugin` in the `webpack.config.js` file. This plugin simplifies the creation of HTML files to serve your Webpack bundles.

```
const HtmlWebpackPlugin = require('html-webpack-plugin');

module.exports = {
    // Other Webpack configurations
    plugins: [
        new HtmlWebpackPlugin({
            template: 'src/index.html'
        })
    ],
};
```

The next step is to automate the inlining of critical CSS. This can be achieved by leveraging the `critical` package directly within the Webpack build process. The integration can be facilitated using the `HtmlWebpackPlugin` events to trigger the extraction and inlining of critical CSS.

To do this, add a custom script in `webpack.config.js` that listens to `HtmlWebpackPlugin`'s `afterEmit` event. Within this event, utilize the `critical` package to extract and inline the critical CSS. The critical package requires specifying the source HTML and the dimensions to consider when determining above-the-fold content.

```
HtmlWebpackPlugin.getHooks(compilation).afterEmit.tapAsync(
    'InlineCriticalCss',
    (data, cb) => {
        critical.generate({
            inline: true,
            base: 'dist/',
            src: 'index.html',
            dimensions: [
                {
                    width: 375,
                    height: 565,
                },
                {
                    width: 1920,
                    height: 1080,
                },
            ],
```

```
18        target: 'index.html',
19      }).then(criticalCss => {
20        cb(null, criticalCss);
21      }).catch(err => {
22        cb(err);
23      });
24    }
25  );
```

This script uses critical.generate function to generate and inline the critical CSS directly into the specified source file. The dimensions option is crucial as it determines the viewport sizes to be considered when generating critical CSS, ensuring that the inlined styles are applicable to various device sizes.

After configuring the Webpack to automate critical CSS inlining, each build will now process the specified HTML files, extract the critical CSS, and inline it within the head tag of the HTML document. This automated process plays a significant role in optimizing web application performance by ensuring that the critical rendering path is as efficient as possible.

```
Output: HTML document with inlined critical CSS.
```

Automating the inlining of critical CSS with Webpack streamlines the performance optimization process, enhancing the initial load time and overall user experience. This advanced technique, when correctly implemented, contributes to building fast, efficient, and scalable web applications.

10.9 Securing Webpack Applications

Securing Webpack applications is crucial for ensuring the integrity and security of the web development process and the resultant web applications. This section outlines key strategies and best practices for securing Webpack applications, including dependency management, configurations, and employing security plugins.

Dependency Management

One of the foundational steps in securing a Webpack application is prudent dependency management. This entails regularly updating dependencies to their latest versions and auditing them for known vulnerabilities.

- **Update Dependencies:** Always keep both Webpack and its plugins updated. Use the npm update command to update the packages to their latest versions.

- **Audit Dependencies:** Use npm audit to scan your project for vulnerabilities within dependencies. This utility will report any known vulnerabilities and suggest updates or patches if available.

Incorporating these practices into the development workflow significantly reduces the risk of including vulnerable packages in your application.

Secure Configurations

Webpack configurations, if not properly secured, can expose applications to various security threats. It is essential to review and secure these configurations.

```
module.exports = {
  // Other configurations...
  mode: 'production',
  devtool: 'source-map',
  output: {
    path: __dirname + '/dist/',
    filename: '[name].[contenthash].js',
    publicPath: '/'
  },
  // Additional configurations...
};
```

In the above configuration snippet, setting mode to 'production' ensures that the built application is optimized and minified, removing debug information and potential security vulnerabilities.

Using contenthash in the output filename can help with cache busting and avoid loading stale, possibly compromised scripts.

Employing Security Plugins

Several Webpack plugins can help improve the security of your application:

- **Webpack Bundle Analyzer:** This plugin helps to visualize and analyze the output bundles. By inspecting the bundle, developers can identify and remove unnecessary dependencies that might include vulnerabilities.

- **Dotenv-webpack:** Use this plugin to securely manage environment variables. It prevents exposing sensitive information and credentials in your Webpack configuration and code.

Integrating these strategies into your Webpack build process not only enhances the security of the application but also instills best practices among development teams for maintaining secure web applications.

Securing Webpack applications is an ongoing process that involves vigilant dependency management, secure configurations, and the judicious use of security-enhancing plugins. By adopting these measures, developers can significantly mitigate risks and safeguard their applications against potential security threats.

10.10 Using Web Workers for Performance Improvements

Web Workers provide a powerful way for web applications to run scripts in background threads, enabling intensive tasks to be performed without interfering with the user interface. This mechanism is particularly beneficial for improving the performance of web applications, as it allows for parallel execution of JavaScript, which is traditionally single-threaded.

To initiate a Web Worker, one must create a new worker script file. This file contains the code the worker will execute, separate from the main JavaScript thread. Consider the following example where a Web Worker is employed to execute a computationally heavy task:

```
1  // main.js - The main JavaScript thread
2  var myWorker = new Worker('worker.js');
3
4  myWorker.onmessage = function(e) {
5      console.log('Message received from worker', e.data);
6  };
7
8  myWorker.postMessage('Hello Worker');
```

The corresponding worker script (worker.js) could be as follows:

```
1  // worker.js - The Web Worker script
2  onmessage = function(e) {
3      console.log('Message received from main script', e.data);
4      var workerResult = 'Result from worker';
5      postMessage(workerResult);
6  };
```

In this setup:

- The main script (main.js) starts the worker and sends it a message using postMessage.

- The worker (worker.js) receives the message, processes it, and sends back a result.

- The main script listens for the message from the worker and reacts to it.

It's important to note that Web Workers operate independently of the main JavaScript thread, meaning that they cannot directly manipulate the DOM. Communication between a Web Worker and the main thread is achieved through the use of messages passed via the postMessage method.

For performance optimization, particularly in the context of large-scale web applications, Web Workers can be utilized for tasks such as:

- Image processing

- Pre-fetching and caching data

- Handling intensive computations that would otherwise block the UI

Furthermore, when using Web Workers within the scope of Webpack, additional considerations must be taken into account. Webpack provides loaders, such as worker-loader, to integrate workers into the build process seamlessly. Here is how one can integrate a Web Worker in a Webpack-configured project:

```
// webpack.config.js
module: {
  rules: [
    {
      test: /\.worker\.js$/,
      use: { loader: 'worker-loader' }
    }
  ]
}
```

This configuration allows for any file ending in .worker.js to be processed by worker-loader, simplifying the inclusion and management of Web Workers in your project. When deployed correctly, Web Workers can significantly enhance the performance and responsiveness of web applications, providing a smoother user experience.

Leveraging Web Workers in the context of Webpack and modern JavaScript applications offers a robust solution for executing background tasks without impacting the performance of the main thread. By understanding and utilizing this technology, developers can ensure their applications remain responsive and efficient, even when performing complex or time-consuming operations.

10.11 Monorepos and Webpack: Managing Large-Scale Projects

Monorepos have gained popularity as a strategy for managing codebases of large-scale projects that consist of multiple interconnected parts. They centralize the code of multiple projects in a single repository, facilitating shared code management, dependency tracking, and streamlined updates. When integrated with Webpack, monorepos can leverage its module bundling capabilities to optimize and manage dependencies across projects efficiently.

Webpack's powerful module resolution system allows for the integration with monorepo architecture through the use of aliases and workspace concepts provided by package managers like Yarn or npm. This integration offers a seamless development experience by enabling code sharing and reuse, which is crucial for maintaining consistency across large projects.

Configuring Webpack for Monorepos

To configure Webpack for use in a monorepo setup, certain adjustments are necessary to handle the complexities of building and managing dependencies across multiple packages or applications within the same repository. This section will provide detailed instructions and code examples to accomplish this configuration.

Firstly, it's essential to ensure that each package or application within the monorepo has its instance of Webpack. This enables independent building and optimization processes tailored to the specific needs of each package while maintaining a central configuration for shared settings and dependencies.

```
1   // Example structure of a Webpack configuration in a monorepo package
2   module.exports = {
3     // Base configuration shared across packages
4     ...
5     resolve: {
6       alias: {
7         // Aliases to enable cross-package imports
8         'shared-components': path.resolve(__dirname, '../../shared-components/src'),

9       ...
10      }
11    },
12    ...
13  };
```

Optimizing Shared Code

One of the main challenges in managing large-scale projects in a monorepo is optimizing the shared code to avoid redundancy and minimize the final bundle size. Webpack offers several features and plugins to tackle this problem effectively.

Utilizing Webpack's `DllPlugin` and `DllReferencePlugin` can significantly reduce initial build times and improve the development workflow. By pre-building dependencies into DLLs (Dynamically Linked Libraries), reusable modules don't need to be processed on every build, speeding up compilation for individual projects.

Additionally, employing code splitting techniques through Webpack's `SplitChunksPlugin` ensures that common dependencies are bundled into shared chunks, reducing the overall size of the application bundles and enhancing the caching strategy for the client-side.

```
1   // Example of using SplitChunksPlugin in a monorepo package
2   module.exports = {
3     optimization: {
4       splitChunks: {
5         chunks: 'all',
6         automaticNameDelimiter: '-',
7         name: true,
8         cacheGroups: {
9           vendors: {
10            test: /[\\/]node_modules[\\/]/,
11            priority: -10
12          },
13          default: {
14            minChunks: 2,
15            priority: -20,
16            reuseExistingChunk: true
17          }
18        }
19      }
20    }
21  };
```

Handling Cross-Package Dependencies

Monorepos often involve cross-package dependencies where one package relies on another within the same repository. To efficiently manage these dependencies without resorting to external package linking tools, Webpack can be configured to resolve imports from local packages directly, streamlining the development process.

```
// Webpack configuration to resolve imports from local packages
resolve: {
  extensions: ['.js', '.jsx', '.ts', '.tsx'],
  alias: {
    'package-a': path.resolve(__dirname, '../../packages/package-a/src'),
    ...
  }
}
```

Managing large-scale projects in a monorepo with Webpack requires a well-thought-out configuration that addresses the challenges of building, optimizing, and maintaining multiple packages within a centralized codebase. By carefully configuring Webpack to handle dependencies, shared code, and cross-package imports, developers can achieve an efficient and scalable setup that benefits from the advantages of both monorepo architecture and Webpack's powerful bundling capabilities.

10.12   Exploring Future Trends in Web Development and Webpack's Role

As the landscape of web development continues to evolve, so too does the technology that powers it. One of the pivotal tools in modern web development is Webpack, whose role and capabilities are in a constant state of adaptation in response to new challenges and opportunities. This section explores the future trends in web development and examines how Webpack is positioned to meet these trends head-on.

The Rise of WebAssembly

One of the most significant trends in web development is the emergence and adoption of WebAssembly (Wasm). WebAssembly allows code written in languages other than JavaScript to run on the web at near-native speed. This opens the door to high-performance web applications that were previously only feasible with traditional, non-web programming languages.

Webpack has begun incorporating support for WebAssembly, enabling developers to integrate Wasm modules into their web applications seamlessly. Here is a brief example of how to include a Wasm module in a Webpack project:

```
module.exports = {
  ///...
  module: {
    rules: [
      {
        test: /\.wasm$/,
        type: 'webassembly/sync',
      },
    ],
  },
  experiments: {
    syncWebAssembly: true,
  },
};
```

Progressive Web Apps (PWAs) and Service Workers

Progressive Web Apps (PWAs) represent another forefront of web development, offering users an app-like experience using only web technologies. Service Workers, which allow for offline functionality, push notifications, and background sync, are a cornerstone of PWAs.

Webpack facilitates the development of PWAs through plugins and loaders that simplify the integration of Service Workers. For instance, the 'WorkboxWebpackPlugin' can be used to add a Service Worker to a Webpack project easily:

```
const WorkboxWebpackPlugin = require('workbox-webpack-plugin');

module.exports = {
```

```
 4    //...
 5    plugins: [
 6        new WorkboxWebpackPlugin.GenerateSW({
 7            clientsClaim: true,
 8            skipWaiting: true,
 9        }),
10    ],
11  };
```

Module Federation and Micro Frontends

The concept of Micro-Frontends – breaking down frontend applications into smaller, more manageable pieces – has gained traction. Module Federation, a feature introduced in Webpack 5, plays a pivotal role in this trend by enabling different frontend applications to share code dynamically at runtime.

This capability is especially beneficial for large, complex applications that are developed by multiple teams. With Module Federation, teams can work independently on separate components or applications, which can then be seamlessly integrated. Here's an example of how Module Federation can be configured in Webpack:

```
 1  module.exports = {
 2      //...
 3      plugins: [
 4          new ModuleFederationPlugin({
 5              name: 'app_name',
 6              filename: 'remoteEntry.js',
 7              exposes: {
 8                  './Component': './src/Component',
 9              },
10          }),
11      ],
12  };
```

Optimization and Asset Management

As applications grow in complexity, optimization, and asset management become critical. Webpack continues to evolve its capabilities in code splitting, tree shaking, and asset optimization to address these needs. Developers can anticipate more sophisticated algorithms and tools for analyzing and optimizing code, as well as enhanced caching strategies for efficient asset management.

The future of web development is bright and full of potential, guided by the continuous evolution of standards, practices, and technologies such as Webpack. Whether it is through supporting emerging technologies like WebAssembly, enhancing the capabilities of Progressive Web Apps, enabling innovative architectural patterns like Module Federation, or pushing the boundaries of optimization, Webpack is set to remain at the forefront of web development. As the ecosystem evolves, so too will Webpack, adapting its features and offerings to meet the ever-changing demands of web development.

www.ingramcontent.com/pod-product-compliance
Lightning Source LLC
LaVergne TN
LVHW022337060326
832902LV00022B/4084